Artificial Intelligence for Risk Management

Other books by Archie Addo published by Business Expert Press

Artificial Intelligence Design and Solution for Risk and Security
ISBN: 9781951527488
https://www.businessexpertpress.com/books/artificial-intelligence-design-and-solution-for-risk-and-security/

Artificial Intelligence for Security
ISBN: 9781951527266
https://www.businessexpertpress.com/books/artificial-intelligence-for-security/

Artificial Intelligence for Risk Management

Archie Addo, Srini Centhala, and
Muthu Shanmugam

BUSINESS EXPERT PRESS

First published in 2020 by
Business Expert Press, LLC
222 East 46th Street, New York, NY 10017
www.businessexpertpress.com

ISBN-13: 978-1-94944-351-6 (paperback)
ISBN-13: 978-1-94944-352-3 (e-book)

Business Expert Press Business Law and Corporate Risk Management Collection

Collection ISSN: 2333-6722 (print)
Collection ISSN: 2333-6730 (electronic)

Cover and interior design by Exeter Premedia Services Private Ltd., Chennai, India

First edition: 2020

10 9 8 7 6 5 4 3 2 1

Printed in the United States of America.

Abstract

The volcano disaster in Hawaii was uncontrollable (Wall Street Journal May 2018) and loss of market shares led to a collapse in the economy of the environment (Pelling et al. 2002; Eddie Guidry et al. 2013). These kinds of uncertainties require some approach to mitigate the situation. Experts are required to identify the associated risks early enough to safeguard the situation and minimize the impact. Here, risk management plays a major role in situations of uncertainty. Relevant questions are: How can this situation be forecasted and taken care of early in similar situations? Can these occurrences be captured historically? Can such patterns of occurrences be identified? Can the data relating to the occurrences be captured? Can the data be used to predict future occurrences? Can the relevance of the data be an important factor? Is security important? What happens if the data are manipulated? How are the data manipulated? How can the data be protected and secured? Security takes an important role in the data and is the driving factor in risk management.

Various types of risk apply to various industries, various business functions, roles, and responsibilities. This book intends to illustrate top business cases and use cases that apply to respective industries by suggesting ways to define, analyze, monitor, control, and mitigate risk. The importance of this approach is to mitigate risk using data and putting corrective action in place. Because humans cannot quickly analyze huge amounts of data, such analysis takes a long time. People can use data science, data analytics, and machine learning (ML) algorithms to speed the process.

Artificial intelligence (AI) enables machines to learn from previous human experiences through data inputs and enables continuous learning from new sets of input data. The development of mathematical algorithms has led to the marked creation of ML, and subsequently to the AI revolution today.

In this *Artificial Intelligence for Risk Management* book, we use AI to mitigate risks through various case studies that will help the reader understand and benefit. AI produces effective and dramatic results in business.

Many organizations desire to understand and improve risk management skills to improve their chances of handling risk.

Recently, risk has become important everywhere because of the large volume of data, different velocity, and variety of data. These aspects of life appear to be growing bigger and more frequent, often accompanied by negative impacts. People can use an undetermined amount of risk to strengthen their position. The range and breadth of risk creates havoc everywhere in the world, and on a variety of projects. Risk management is important in an organization because without it, the organization may have trouble defining its objectives. However, the most important strategy implementation is fear of financial loss. This book focuses on problem statements with appropriate use cases and proposes AI solutions using data science and machine learning approaches.

In this book, we hope to provide concrete answers to the crucial questions facing so many organizations: Where are these risks and what can be done to lower their impacts? Is AI part of the answers to the risk mitigations?

Keywords

project management; construction management; program management; skills development; risk; artificial intelligence; analytics; ML; mitigation; performance review; data science, and business intelligence

Contents

Acknowledgments

Our artificial intelligence (AI) and risk expert colleagues across the world have worked in the corporate world to acquire knowledge and expertise. AI and risk researchers and practitioners have had a profound impact on our thinking and on the contents of this book. Subsequently, working with many corporate customers and serving them has greatly influenced the preparation of this material.

Thanks to our parents, Godson Addo, Mary (Vanderpuije) Addo, Seetharaman Centhala, Thulasi Centhala, K. Shanmugam, and S. Saroja, for encouraging us to get an education and work diligently in the field of our work. We do not think we would have made it this far without their support.

We would like to extend great thanks to our families—Louvaine Addo, Mala Srini, Kavitha Muthu—and Archie's and Srini children: Koushik Seethula, Shashank Seethula, Srima Seethula—Muthu's children: Maanasa Muthu, Sarvesh Muthu—for their collective patience with our busy schedules.

Thanks to Editide for copyediting. We would like to extend great thanks to Venkat and everyone at Bizstats Technologies Pvt. Ltd. who enabled us to be Software-as-a-Service (SaaS) BizStats.AI company, which provided one of the major inputs to write this book.

CHAPTER 1

Introduction

- Target audience
- What you can get from this book?
- What this book covers
- This book's mind map
- Organization of chapters
  - Introduction to Artificial Intelligence (AI)
  - Introduction to Risk
  - Introduction to the AI Knowledge Base
  - Business Use Cases
  - AI Solutions for Risk
- Conclusion
- References

Chapter Outline

- Book Introduction
- Organization of the Book
- Chapter Introduction

Key Learning Points
  - Learn and understand: introduction

Target Audience

This book mainly focuses on artificial intelligence (AI) and how managers can apply AI to risk management. This book follows current trends in AI in the branch of Natural Language Processing , Natural Language

Question and Answering System of AI, Conversational AI in risk domains, AI supporting drones, AI cybersecurity, Internet of Things (IoT) devices, and use cases.

Each applicable AI topic targets:

- Corporate top executives, founders, Chief Technology Officers, Chief Information Officers, Chief Data Officers, Chief Security Officers, Chief Risk Officers, data scientists, data architects, AI designers, AI engineers, project managers, and consultants to understand how to manage risk using AI.
- Students, teachers, and developers will find this book useful and practical. It will provide an overview of many AI components, and introduce how it can be used in corporate environments, start-ups, large-, medium-, and small-sized companies.
- Anybody who strives to understand how AI can be used for risk.

What Can You Get From This Book?

- Understand and learn about AI and how to apply AI to risk.
- Design and apply knowledge-based AI solutions to solve risk-related problems.
- Architecting and designing AI applied systems that mostly rely on the following:
  - Subject Matter Experts. Those with a practical view of how solutions can be used, not just developed. Here, risk provides an example using case studies in the book.
  - Appropriate applied mathematics and algorithms are used in the book. Do not skip the mathematical equations if you have the need to study them. It is important to note that AI relies heavily on mathematics.
  - Applied physics and usage into hardware systems and futuristic approaches from quantum computers to parallel processing of networks in quantum computer handlings. AI is still evolving with many new areas of possible opportuni-

ties. Give your full attention to new concepts and applied creative ideas in the Futuristic AI chapter.

- Decision theory, decision-making process, the Markov Decision Process algorithm.

What This Book Covers

This book covers mainly an introduction to AI and how it is applied in corporations, start-ups, large-, medium-, and small-sized companies, to help automate the tedious jobs of mitigating risk. This book will help those in organizations' working environment (as a resource), applying and automating AI and ML to help human experts.

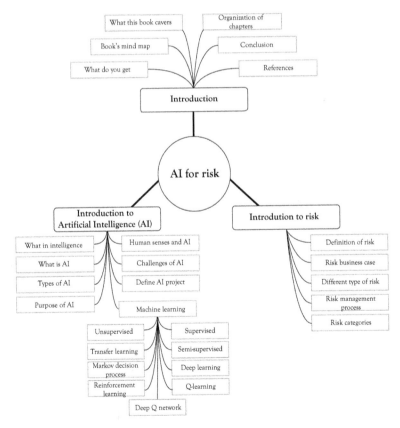

Figure 1.1 Mind map of the book

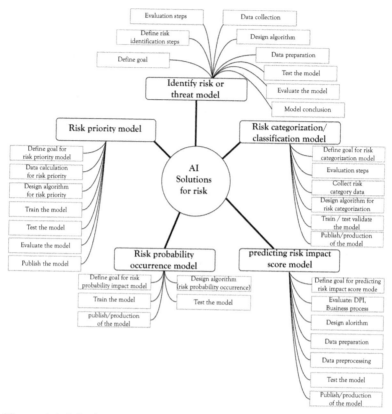

Figure 1.2 Mind map of artificial intelligence solutions for risk

- How to get true value from AI?
- What are the visionary business use cases for AI?
- How do I identify the best business case to adopt AI and evaluate opportunities?
- Should I build or buy an AI platform?
- How do I find and recruit top AI talent for my enterprise?
- How will I bring AI into my business to increase revenue or decrease costs?
- How can I facilitate AI adoption in my organization?

Especially when dealing with data that include data collection, data preparation, data transformation, securing the data, using the data to align organizational AI, use cases, and much more. Figure 1.1 provides a mind map to give the reader an idea of what is covered in this book and the organization of the chapters.

Figure 1.2 provides a mind map of AI Solutions for Risk. This figures gives the reader a sense of which risk areas are covered with AI solutions in this book.

CHAPTER 2

Introduction to Artificial Intelligence

- Introduction to artificial intelligence (AI)
- Types of AI
- AI and purpose

Chapter Outline

- Define intelligence
- Define AI
- Types of AI
- Purpose of AI
- Human senses
- Define an AI project

Key Learning Points
- Learn and understand machine learning

Introduction to Artificial Intelligence (AI)

What Is Intelligence?

Intelligence is the ability to understand or deduce information and retain it as knowledge, and subsequently apply it toward a context in an environment (Barrat 2013). This includes logic, self-awareness, learning, emotional knowledge, reasoning, planning, creativity, and problem solving. Intelligence can be found in humans and animals. This intelligence is expected to extend to machines and that is what strong artificial intelligence (AI) is about. This book expands from basic to advanced AI.

What Is AI?

People all over the world provide definitions of AI. Here are some definitions of AI. AI is the science- and engineering-enabling intelligence, specifically in computer programs, using computers to understand human intelligence and other living things. About 60 years ago, John McCarthy called on a group of computer scientists to discern if computers could learn like a child (McCarthy 1959). The project objective was to see if computers could solve all sorts of problems that are reserved for humans and to improve themselves, especially when addressing a huge amount of data. Since then AI has been in university laboratories and super-secret labs. In 1955, McCarthy defined AI as having seven characteristics:

1. Simulating higher functions of the human brain.
2. Programming a computer to use general language.
3. Arranging hypothetical neurons in a manner so it can form concepts.
4. Finding ways to determine and measure problem complexity.
5. Self-improvement.
6. Abstraction that defines the quality of addressing ideas rather than events.
7. Randomness and creativity.

McCarthy further discussed that all the various parts of learning and intelligence can be precisely described as intelligence that a machine can be built to simulate.

In 1995, Jake Copeland described AI further, averring that AI has no technical concepts. He analyzed what those working in AI must achieve before claiming to have built a thinking machine. Copeland further itemized areas in AI as follows:

- Generalize learning
- Recognize human faces
- Reason to draw conclusions based on information gathered
- Problem solving
- Give way to humans

Other people defined AI as computers that seem like they have human intelligence. Not merely the ability to obey road signs and drive forward, rather to show human emotions such as road rage. This is not a new concept; one can recall Dortmund Professor McCarthy who coined the term AI in 1956.

Recently, a huge amount of data is being generated. Technology giants such as Google, Facebook, Twitter, Microsoft, Amazon, and IBM embrace AI to solve problems of various magnitudes. AI is being used in robotics to solve complex empirical problems. AI can manifest in many ways such as forecasting the weather, based on the data from its source. However, the same data can yield a different forecast, based on the intent of the question. Thus, it is capable of thinking, based on how it is programmed. NLP makes this more exotic. One of the most exciting areas of AI is machine learning (ML). Machines can retain knowledge based on the data collected, in contrast to a human who retain knowledge and respond differently.

Types of AI

There are three types of AI: Weak, Strong, and Superintelligence (AI researcher Ben Goertzel 2014). Weak AI focuses on narrow tasks. Strong AI can apply intelligence to solve problems generally rather than focusing on one specific problem. AI has the intelligence to respond with intelligence and can be compared to a typical human. Superintelligence AI is supposed to have intelligence attributes that surpass those of the brightest and most gifted human minds (Muehlhauser May 2014). Its recursive self-improvement provides a rapid outcome able to create artificial general intelligence.

AI and Capabilities

The field of AI is vast and yet recognizes many unknowns. Some known AI capabilities are listed as follows (Brownlee 2013):

- NLP enables machines to communicate in natural way in human languages.
- Knowledge representation enables machines to represent known knowledge.
- Automated reasoning enables machines to determine appropriate reasoning like a human.

- ML entails teaching the machines.
- Computer vision enables machines to see and detect.
- Robotics helps in automating movable use cases such as manufacturing units.
- Internet of Things (IoT) devices help in data collection and controlling machines through sensors.
- Virtual reality helps in simulating human senses close to reality. Make your mind believe.

What Is the Purpose of AI?

- To better humankind.
- To help humans extend their capabilities on repeated tasks through automation.
- To avoid human and manual errors on repeated tasks.
- To improve programmatic approaches to align with ever-changing business demands and requirements. Instead of programmatically maintaining business rules to data-driven decision processes, accommodates business demands immediately.
- To handle the large volume of data generated every day, using approximately 2.5 billion gigabytes.
- To handle a variety of data in an automated way.
- To handle the velocity of data.
- To detect patterns in data.
- No human or group of humans can handle the huge volume of data and the variety of data at its present velocity of accumulation.

Human Senses

The five senses of humans are sight, sound, touch, smell, and taste. Currently, machines are capable of replicating the sight sense through a camera to see and project through monitors and projectors. Machines can replicate the sound sense through a microphone to listen. Speakers speak through speakers, users touch screens, keyboards, and mouse. People have yet to develop machines that have a sense of smell and taste. However, a couple of new inventions are being developed such as a digital nose and smell maker, as well as an electronic tongue to mimic the taste sense. People are working to answer the challenges associated with new technological machine and device capabilities. Artifacts are still evolving, and reliability and usability are not tested yet on real-world applications. Acceptance among users is still unclear. Applying machines with these digital senses to real-world applications is an enormous accomplishment, although they are still in the research and development (R&D) experimental phase. These kinds of risks are very high, and one corporation alone cannot handle these challenges. That is why many developers are using open source environments and conducting university-based projects. It is unclear how reliable and secure capabilities will be to avoid early detection in the new evolving technologies.

The Horizontal and Vertical AI landscapes. Horizontal AI focuses on general questions and fundamental problems across industries. Large corporations such as Google, Facebook, Microsoft, Amazon, IBM, and universities are investing in Horizontal AI. Vertical AI focuses on a specific industry problem, specific business case, and use cases. Many startups and medium-sized companies are investing in and exploring Vertical AI.

Some major Horizontal AI projects are Watson (IBM), AlphaGo (Google), Google Brain, Blue Brain (IBM), M (Facebook), Siri (Apple), Google Now, Cortana (Microsoft), Wolfram Alpha (Wolfram Research), Echo (Amazon), and Google home.

Some of the Vertical AI projects are www.BizStats.AI—Retail E-Commerce and Event Ticket.

Here is the list of supported industry-specific verticals:

- Retail e-commerce Analytics AI: https://bizstats.ai/solutions/by_industry/retail_e-commerce.html
- Automotive Analytics AI: https://bizstats.ai/solutions/by_industry/automotive.html
- Banking and Financing Analytics AI: https://bizstats.ai/solutions/by_industry/banking_finance.html
- Consumer Products Analytics AI: https://bizstats.ai/solutions/by_industry/consumer_products.html

Define AI Projects

An AI project is similar to PMBoK (PMI 2017) project definition except that AI projects are more dependent on data and algorithms, such as the availability of initial data for training, continuing data collection strategy, cleaning up collected data, determining the useful features of data, transforming data to fit a model, selecting appropriate algorithms, evaluating multiple algorithms to determine accuracy, comparing against other algorithms, and determining the learning rate of the model. Can this model function autonomously or does it need human intelligence to speed up the learning process?

The first phase of an AI Project is the most important. It defines and identifies business cases and use cases like a regular project, but has more risk associated with it. Because AI projects are still in the discovery mode and processes are still evolving, companies are trying to learn from each other's mistakes, challenges, and new knowledge, determining how to

Figure 2.1 AI project value proposition

monetize. Again, this falls into the business value proposition like a regular project. See Figure 2.1.

AI project value propositions include great business value, causing an abrupt increase in revenue in the shortest time possible by gaining more customers to increase market share, in the mode of start-up companies. AI projects are continuous, collecting a new set of data and applying predefined/preselected algorithms and pretrained models that have already gone through the initial training. The goal is to reach success with great accuracy, near to 80 percent or more. The required accuracy is based on the business case, the goal of the project, and the problem. For example, the AI self-driving car project needs nearer to 100 percent accuracy and has zero fault tolerance. This is because human safety is directly involved. But some other AI projects, such as assistance provided by Apple's SIRI project may not need 100 percent accuracy. In general, more accuracy with less fault tolerance is better.

AI projects need the latest trends and demanding roles, skill sets such as those of data scientists, data architects, data designers, data engineers, ML engineers, AI engineers, cloud engineers, and subject matter experts in their respective fields. In addition to human resources, machines are also part of the resources needed such as IoT devices, virtual reality devices, robots, and others.

See Figure 2.2 for AI-based projects and AI Products that enable business value creation. Using AI will provide more value that is data driven and automated.

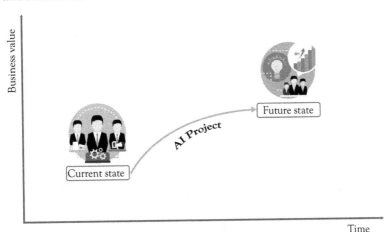

Figure 2.2 Business value versus time

Business value is the net quantifiable benefit that may be tangible, intangible, or both. Business value benefits can include time, money, goods, or intangibles.

Most corporations strive for the following business value:

- How to safeguard and increase monetary assets.
- How to increase market share and revenue share.
- How to increase the customer base by designing innovative useful products.
- How to increase the good will of the organization.
- How to improve brand recognition, brand value, and corporate reputation.
- How to improve customer experience.

Big Data Ecosystem

The big data ecosystem is growing exponentially, meaning more data are being generated every minute and usage of data devices, data collectors, data aggregators, and data users or buyers is increasing. In the big data ecosystem, a need exists for AI solutions for risk. See Figure 2.3. The risk

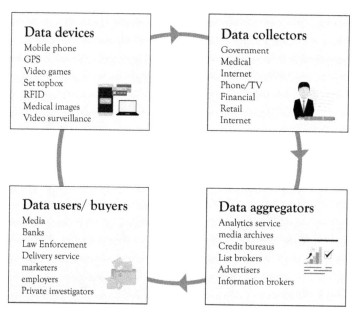

Figure 2.3 Big data ecosystem

associated with AI projects is enormous. AI projects have positive risks and negative risks. The next section details some positive and negative risks of AI projects.

Positive and Negative Risks of AI

One major challenge and a negative risk of AI is to align with human emotions and safety. It is presumed that AI is programmed to do something that is overwhelming. If AI gets into the hands of the wrong person, it can be used to create harm, such as serving as a weapon. AI arms can lead to AI war, which may cause mass casualties. Weapons could be designed to be extremely difficult to turn off, causing humans to lose control of the situation (Eliezer Yudkowsky 2008).

Humans may have only good intentions when developing AI systems, but the system itself may develop a destructive method to achieve its intended goal. In such a situation, much havoc can ensue. For example, requesting a vehicle to take a person from Point A to Point B very fast might create problems because an AI machine may travel too fast. Many other examples can be added to this scenario. The point here is that AI systems must be made with considerations for human safety.

Well-known people in science and technology have expressed concerns about AI: Stephen Hawking, Elon Musk, Steve Wozniak, and Bill Gates. Initially, strong AI may take a long time to develop, but recent accomplishments with AI has provide concern that the acceleration of AI development can move at a surprising pace if humans do not take the necessary precautions to protect the development of strong AI. AI can become more intelligent than any human and ultimately humans cannot predict how it will behave. Presently, humans control the world and to have something else controlling the world is a scary thought. Thus, the idea is to support AI safety and with great caution.

Negative Risks of AI

- No standardized terminology exists, and AI can loosely be viewed as a machine that chooses whatever action appears to best achieve its goals. This means AI can choose whatever function it assesses as best, depending on the mathematical algorithm.

- The goal of the AI system may not be intelligent enough to think of resisting programmer attempts to modify it and may not be sufficiently advanced to react rationally. This lack of oversight may lead to resisting any changes to its goal structure.
- A super-intelligent program created by humans may be obedient to humans. However, it may be more intelligent than a human, thereby understanding the moral truth of humans more than humans. This could create a problem slowing it down, simply because it knows more than the human, and may think it knows the best approach.
- Using AI to do things for humans may lead to losing our skills.
- Humans will end up blaming machines for a mistake made by humans.
- A smart machine may decide that humans are not needed.
- AI may use human weaknesses against us.
- AI may use human intentions against humans.

Positive Risks of AI

- AI can now automate everyday tasks.
- AI can help with management decisions and put the most effective teams together.
- AI can process and analyze a huge amount of data.
- AI can converse with customers to resolve customer issues.
- AI can create algorithms to forecast growth.
- AI can help doctors diagnose patients.
- Incorporating AI into an organization is like having a private robotic assistant that can streamline the work that needs to be undertaken in the office space.
- AI can be quite productive.

- AI can carry out menial tasks in the office such as managing referrals.
- AI can update and coordinate schedules.
- Some predictors speculate that AI is not yet mature enough to provide careful assessment of its value to the organization.
- Planning for the inclusion of AI into organizational capabilities can be handled in an orderly and beneficial fashion with a little planning effort.
- AI technology is changing at a fast rate. Organizations are now in various stages of managing their AI interests.

Challenges of AI and Adoption

Distraction of AI

Many organizations are distracted by the following issues, attributed to AI:

Organizations are concerned that not enough attention is being focused on the dangers of AI. The fact that many devices are being hooked to the Internet, it is creating fear that the data generated from the devices may cause problems in terms of cybersecurity issues. Besides, there are not enough skilled cyber workers. It is being predicted that using AI and ML could automate threat detection and response. There is a possibility that this approach could be the response to a potential threat and likely be more efficient (Ford February 11, 2015).

Many organizations are suspicious of data risk issues. However, ML algorithms could create a false sense of security. Quite recently, researchers have trained supervised ML software. Algorithms to train the machine learner must be well defined. Rolled out software requires thorough scrubbing of anomalous data points. The algorithm may miss some attacks. Attackers who get access to corporate systems could corrupt data by switching labels so that some malware is tagged as clean code. Algorithms that are compromised and do not flag a problem can cause bigger risk issues.

In addition to all the risk issues discussed, AI and ML should not be used for risk defense. An appropriate risk process must be in place to monitor and minimize the risk associated with algorithm adoption and ML. Researchers showed that a challenge persists in finding resources with knowledge and experience in cybersecurity and data.

Mass Unemployment Due to AI Adoption

It is typical in the United States that people stop working at the age of 65 and spend their time mentoring other workers or volunteering. In the manufacturing sector, AI may not have a negative impact on losses. Job losses may come in the service sectors, such as construction, health care, and business. The loss of a job will mostly depend on how jobs will be transformed by adding new tasks while being supported by computers and robots.

AI algorithms are replacing jobs that are routine, repetitive, and take much time and thus are more easily and effectively performed by machines and robots. This means humans can be left to tackle interpersonal, social, and emotional jobs (Furman December 20, 2016). A typical example is that the bank teller job may change so tellers will concentrate on giving money and helping clients.

Areas in which AI and ML can be greatly helpful are agriculture, weather forecasting, and determining the latest market prices. A typical requirement for an online customer is requesting help to purchase products. AI can add services to improve customer experiences, allowing companies to retain those customers.

It is possible that human labor may be less expensive than machines. There may be a lack of required skill, poor energy, poor energy infrastructure, broadband, and transport networks. Other areas such as legal and regulatory issues could use AI quite well. When AI is deployed, the doctor needs to confirm if the AI is responsible for claims of medical malpractice.

The Impossibility of Total Human Control

AI is currently popular and can be heard everywhere. Many business sectors use AI including insurance, health care, genetics, agriculture industry, road traffic management, and other areas that are based on data. Some people believe companies are trying to remove human resources from routine work and replace them with AI and ML. Many organizations like what AI can do for them. Yet, other companies focus on negative aspects such as data risk issues, data privacy concerns, mass unemployment due to AI integration, unbiasedness of AI, the impossibility of total human control, and the notion that AI-based solutions are still too expensive for most organizations. There is a question of whether real problems exist in using AI or simply being prejudice against the application and idea that it brings to the business market.

AI has been used and recommended by many experts in business and computing fields.

AI and ML use large amounts of data. Most of these data are personal. Recently, data have leaked from organizations such as Facebook and Apple. These organizations use ML for personal data processing. Is it possible that AI and ML will increase the probability of data leakage? However, no cases have occurred of AI data leak; organizations build AI to solve data leak problems.

Usually, top-notch designers design AI software, making the application safe and difficult to hack. If the software were hacked, it would be difficult to understand and make changes to it. The data in AI or neural networks cannot be decrypted because of the way they are built. Subsequently, AI systems and neural network systems are developed using open source frameworks and libraries such as Microsoft CNTK, Theano, TensorFlow, Caffe, Keras, and Torch. Most of these open source frameworks are supported by large organizations such as Google, Facebook, and Microsoft. The supporting organizations have policies that ensure privacy through penetration tests. Of the five causes of data breach, four come from a human error that stems from password error. This means that problems related to AI are not legitimate concerns and can be considered myths. Data leaks will diminish drastically if organizations pay more attention to train their staff with the basic rules of data management.

People do not like their data to be analyzed in fear of being targeted. Personal data analyses have been performed in insurance, finance, and other industries. People fear that other people or machines will know their private details, which creates fear in them. AI alone does not violate any personal data policies. However, data insights reveal organization status to show profit or loss. Organizations developing AI have processes to regulate documentation and personal data. Further, people fear that AI and the neural network will replace managers in making decisions. Every organization is interested in skillful and loyal personnel. The existence of AI and neural networks does not mean companies have plans to substitute humans with computers, even though computers can do the work of the human faster and probably better. Gartner predicted that, in 2020, AI will generate 2.3 million jobs from 1.8 million jobs.

AI programs and robots are liable to make mistakes. A good example can be cited with a case of robot failing exam questions that would be obvious to young children. Police departments have used AI systems and those systems can also make mistakes. This can be concerning, such as distinguishing between a toy gun and a real gun.

People have some level of fear that a smart computer with AI will control humans instead of the other way around. This belief stems mostly from customers who think about dealing with computers rather than humans after watching sci-fi movies. This further raises the following questions:

- Complex AI systems comprise a few subsystems such as speech recognition, decision making, and data analysis. All the subsystems are hard coded; thus, it is not possible for the subsystems to add new features by themselves.
- AI systems have limitations based on how they are developed.
- Developing AI that is close to a human can be quite expensive to have and maintain.

Developers can create very complex neural networks and ML algorithms for various industries. However, the cost of such systems is high and difficult. Complexity grows with new product ideas.

Data to AI

Let us illustrate how AI operates: AI starts with data and progresses to data science, then to ML, deep learning, and finally to AI. Figure 2.4 shows the relationship between data, data science, ML, deep learning, and AI.

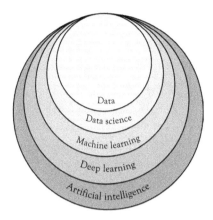

Figure 2.4 Data to AI

The distinction between data, data science, ML, deep learning, and AI is defined next.

What Are Data?

Data are information usually used for analysis, calculation, or to plan something. Data are often produced or stored by a computer. Data have value and relate to subjects that are qualitative or quantitative. Data explore the study and construction of algorithms that can learn from data and make decisions and predictions or decisions by building a model. ML is a subset of AI in the field of computer science and data science.

Examples of data in the corporate world are revenue, sales data, profits, and stock prices. In the government sector, examples are rates such as crime rates and unemployment rates. Examples in the nongovernmental sector are the number of homeless people or the top location of homeless people.

What Is Data Science?

Data science is the field that uses scientific methods, processes, algorithms, and systems to derive knowledge and insights from acquired data in an environment. Data can be structured or unstructured. The idea of data science is to unify statistics, data analysis, ML, and related methods to provide insights.

What Is ML?

ML was first coined by Arthur Samuel in 1959. ML explores the study and construction of algorithms that can learn from data and make decisions and predictions by building a model. ML is a subset of AI in the field of computer science and data science. ML is used in a range of computing tasks that require designing and programming explicit algorithms. ML means simply teach machines to accomplish expected tasks.

Major Problems of Teaching Machines

Major problems in teaching machines are:

- Identifying methods to teach the machines.
- Identifying, collecting, and preparing training data.
- It takes much time to train machines.
- Training machines needs many computational resources.
- ML requires improving model accuracy with efficient time and optimal resources.

Types of ML Systems

The types of ML systems are very important to choose, based on the use cases, type of available algorithms, types of data, and problem one is trying to solve. Listed as follows are the most commonly used types of ML systems:

- Supervised ML
- Unsupervised ML
- Semisupervised ML
- Transfer ML
- Reinforcement ML
- Ensemble learning

Additionally, types of ML can be categorized based on how the machine is trained. Training is based on offline learning or online (real-time) learning in a predefined batch mode or stream mode with regular intervals.

- Offline learning

- Online learning
- Batch mode learning
- Stream mode learning

Another way to categorize ML systems is based on similarity and derived from mathematical models.

- Instance-based learning is how similar the new set of data is coming in and detecting new patterns on data that enable continuous learning.
- Model-based learning derives from mathematical formulas to construct a mathematical model.

What Is Supervised ML?

Supervised ML is a way to teach machines through training data by examples with input and output of historically collected data or valid data labeled by humans. The name supervised ML reflects concept of supervised by humans to improve high accuracy to address problems of classification or categorization. Further, the goal is to predict the future value of continuous variables such as predicting housing prices, based on available historical data by applying appropriate algorithms to extend mathematically and geometrically from the historical data points linearly or nonlinearly.

Linear Versus Nonlinear

Here are explanations of linear and nonlinear data points. This is the starting point for determining a pattern in the data that is either linear or nonlinear. Linear patterns are any data points that are in these patterns (x,y) = (0,0),(1,1),(2.2),(3,3). See Figure 2.5.

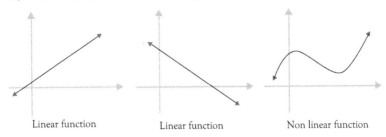

Linear function   Linear function   Non linear function

Figure 2.5 Linear and nonlinear graphs

Some of the important and famous supervised machine algorithms are:

- k-nearest neighbors, a nonparametric method used to classify and regress.
- Linear regression is a linear approach to modeling the relationship between a dependent variable and one or more explanatory independent variables.
- Logistic regression is a method of analyzing a dataset with one or more independent variables that determine an outcome.
- Support Vector Machines are supervised ML algorithms used for classification or regression challenges.
- Decision trees and random forests are collections of decision trees whose results are aggregated into one result.
- Neural networks are a series of algorithms that recognize underlying relationships in a set of data through a process that imitates the way the human brain operates.

Some typical use cases for supervised ML algorithms follow:

- Classification of customers based on purchasing patterns, behavior patterns, frequency patterns, income-based patterns, and so on.
- Grouping of customers by lifetime value usage patterns.
- Predicting customer churn based on usage pattern, value versus price, competitor pricing strategy on campaigns, introducing new products and services, and much more.
- Fraud detection by analyzing data to find anomalies, unique patterns, and extreme cases.
- Sales forecasts and predictions.
- Risk identification and risk categorization.
- Building and categorizing threat models.

What Is Unsupervised ML?

Unsupervised ML describes a type of teaching machine through training data autonomously without labeled data. The name unsupervised ML reflects the concept of being unsupervised by humans by extending algorithms to approximate groupings, identifying the association between data and anomaly detection.

Some important and famous unsupervised machine algorithms are:

- Clustering
- Association rule
- Anomaly detection
- Dimensionality reduction
- Some of typical use cases for unsupervised ML algorithms are:
- Clustering or grouping of any data.
- Anomaly detection of any set of data.
- Similar product and associated product recommendation.
- Feature reduction on high dimensional data.

What Is Semisupervised ML?

Semisupervised ML is a type of ML with some part using a supervised learning method and some part using an unsupervised learning method in any combination of labeled and unlabeled data. Typically, semisupervised ML applies the unsupervised ML algorithm first for unlabeled data and identifies labeled data and applies supervised learning algorithms to improve accuracy. Sometimes, annotation tools are also used to complete human labeling through web-based applications such as http://bizstats. ai/product/urAI.html

bizstats.ai

urAI—Annotation Tool | BizStats.AI

Event tickets Application Programming Interface (API) improves user's search experience by a Named Entity Recognition ML model, exclusively for event ticketing sites.

What Is Deep Learning?

Deep learning is part of ML methods based on useful data representations or features from the raw data. Data representations are meant to be the understanding of the data structures and identify, extract, and evolve underlying features from the raw data. The feature's learning can

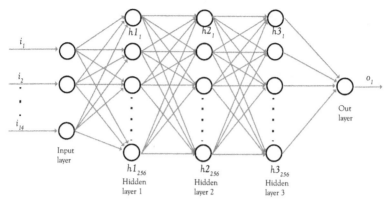

Figure 2.6 *Fully connected neural network layer*

be supervised learning, semisupervised learning, unsupervised learning, or reinforcement learning. Different deep learning architectures are artificial neural networks, deep neural networks, deep belief networks, and recurrent neural networks based on learning data representations.

Typical distinctions between traditional ML approaches and deep learning approaches are that deep learning extracts automatic learning features from the raw data using deep learning models formed by different types of layers.

Fully connected neural network layers consist of a list of inputs inserted in a list of outputs (see Figure 2.6). There are three basic types of layers: (1) input layer, (2) output layer, and (3) hidden layer. Some functionality-based layers are the convolution layer, max/avg pooling layer, dropout layer, nonlinearity layer, and loss function layer.

Convolution Neural Networks

Convolution Neural Network (CNN) consists of a convolution layer that filters input section by section for useful features and flows through all sections to automatically extract the important features for the given problem. CNN works best in image recognition use cases. See the following illustration:

Perceptron (P): 2 input layer → 1 output layer.

The perceptron is the basic architecture of artificial neural networks.

Let us consider, X1, X2, X3 … Xn as inputs and W1, W2, W3 … Wn as weights

X1 → W1

X2 → W2

X3 → W3

Xn → Wn

and Weighted Sum $z= w1x1+w2x2+w3x3 \ldots\ldots +wnxn= w^T.x$

$$h(x)= step(w^T.x)= step(z)$$

Feed forward (FF): 2 input layer → 2 hidden layer → 1 output layer.

Radial basis network (RBF): 2 input layer → 2 hidden layer → output layer.

Deep feed forward (DFF): 3 input layer → 2 hidden layer → 1 output layer.

Recurrent Neural Network (RNN): 3 input layer → 2 hidden layer → 3 output layer.

Long/Short Term Memory (LSTM): 3 input layer → 2 hidden layers with memory cell → 3 output layer.

Gated Recurrent Unit (GRU): 3 input layer → 2 hidden layers with different memory cell → 3 output layer.

Auto encoder (AE): 4 input layer → 1 hidden layer → 4 output layer with a matched number of input cells to output cells.

Variational AE (VAE): 4 input layer → 1 hidden layer with probabilistic hidden cell → 4 output layer with a matched number of inputs to output cells.

De-noising AE (DAE): 4 input layers with noisy input cell → 1 hidden layer → 4 output layer with a matched number of inputs to the output cells.

Sparse AE (SAE): 2 input layer → 1 hidden layer

Deep learning has been applied to image recognition, computer vision, speech recognition, natural language processing, machine translations, and much more. Most recently, deep learning has become very popular in the technology industry in the following areas of computer assistance—human language translations, customer support, bots, and much more—explored while writing this book.

As to AI for risk, we used most deep learning architectures to automatically detect features from raw data to apply respective use cases for risk. These are covered in the AI solutions for risk chapters.

What Is Transfer Learning?

Transfer learning focuses on storing knowledge from solving one problem and applying it to another or similar problems. A typical example is knowledge gained from recognizing one thing and applying it to a similar thing.

Transfer learning is a type of transfer knowledge gained through previously trained models and then applying additional training to answer a specific problem as an add-on. The goal is to use a previously trained model for a similar problem and to train the model to extend the solution to other problems.

A typical example is in natural language processing applications. Some models were trained with the English language corpus, the knowledge gained from recognizing English words and grammar, and then applying that knowledge to act as a chatbot with additional training toward specific use-case-based problems, making it a chatbot.

What Is Reinforcement Learning?

Reinforced learning is the part of ML that relates to how software agents are supposed to act in some environments to maximize reward. Disadvantages related to reinforced learning usage accrue from its generality. Researchers study this aspect in game theory, control theory, operations research, and statistics. Reinforced learning is different from standard supervised learning in correct input/output pairs.

Reinforcement learning consists of a learning agent that continuously learns from observing and trying out the next action, based on the defined policy. The machine earns rewards or penalties and, based on the real-time examples or tryouts, automatically updates policies. The machine continues these steps until the optimal policy is constructed.

Markov Decision Process

How does one apply Markov Decision Process (MDP) to automate the decision-making process?

MDPs comes from the Russian mathematician named Andrew Markov, going back to 1950.

MDP provides a mathematical approach for making decisions in situations with output that are partly random and partly under the control of a decision maker. MDP has been used to study optimizing problems using dynamic programming and reinforcement learning. People in many disciplines use MDP such as robotics, automatic control, manufacturing, economics, applying gaming, and driverless cars, and it can be extended to risk use cases.

MDP can be better explained using a scenario where the thought process is applied as an agent. In the case of the ML model, the thought process uses a calculation that goes through the trial-and-error process. In summary, MDP is a sequential decision for a fully observable, random environment (MDP). This environment consists of a set of states, a set of actions and rewards, that includes positive and negative rewards. The policy will be captured to maintain different possible states (s0, s1, s2, ... sn), all possible actions from the current state to the new state [A(s0), A(s1), A(s2), ... A(sn)], and respective rewards, which is R(s). The policy is represented as $\pi(s)$.

MDP is explored in detail in the coming chapters and is illustrated as follows:

- A probability to move to different states.
- A way to evaluate rewards to being in different states.

$s \in S$ —a set of states

$a \in A$ —a set of actions

$T(s,a,s')$—a transition function/model/dynamics

prob that aa from ss leads to s′s′, that is, $P(s'|a,s)P(s'|a,s)$

$R(s,a,s')R(s,a,s')$ —a reward(cost) function aka $R(s')R(s')$ or $R(s)R(s)$ to maximize the reward/cost.

α —a start state

γ —a discount factor

MDPs are nondeterministic/stochastic search problems (Haskell May 10, 2019). Nondeterministic means that next action could be anything, in any direction, and not in the predefined sequence of steps. Each time it goes to a different state that is not in sequence, it may not be the same.

State transition is represented as an equation, for a Markov state s and successor state "s," the state transition probability is defined by PSS'=P[St+1=s'|St=s].

Two approaches to agent learning are active learning and passive learning. Passive learning mainly focuses on learning the possibility of the environment and exploration, whereas active learning builds policy by acting.

Decision Toward Next Action

MDP process use cases mainly rest on the decision to determine the next action for the use cases listed as follows:

- Robot path planning
- Route planning
- Aircraft navigation
- Driverless car navigation
- Manufacturing process
- Network switching and routing

Monte Carlo

The Monte Carlo (MC) algorithm is based on the small probability concept of the randomization algorithm, which applies randomness and applies the statistics of standard normal distribution. It uses repeated random sampling to get approximation solutions. This method is used in a case with no analytical solutions or numerical solutions.

Steps to implement MC methods follow:

1. Determine the properties of statistics of input data.
2. Generate all possible inputs based on the identified properties of statistics in Step 1.
3. Perform a deterministic calculation.
4. Analyze statistical results.

MC Simulation

MC simulation is a computerized mathematical technique to account for risk in the quantitative analysis and decision-making process. An MC simulation is a useful tool to predict future results by calculating a formula multiple times with different random inputs.

This method can solve many optimization problems and numerical problems by generating sampling from statistical distribution input data to simulate working systems and predict financial investments with risk analysis to theoretical physics problems.

$$I = \int_0^{\inf} \frac{e^{-x}}{1 + (x-1)^2} dx$$

Because the integral part ranges from 0 to infinite, this needs a numerical approximation.

Crude MC

This crude method of calculating approximation uses the following formula:

$$f_{ave} = \frac{1}{b-a} \int_a^b f(x)dx$$

Determine variance of estimation:

$$\sigma^2 = \left\langle I^2 \right\rangle - \left\langle I \right\rangle^2$$

Determine variance of estimation expanded:

$$\sigma^2 = [\frac{b-a}{N} \sum_i^N f^2(x_i)] - [\sum_j^N \frac{b-a}{N} f^2(x_j)]^2$$

Common probability distributions are:

- Normal/bell curve
- Lognormal
- Uniform
- Triangular

Most business activities, plans, and processes are too complex for an analytical solution. Many business situations involve uncertainty in many dimensions. For example, variable market demand, unknown plans of competitors, uncertainty in costs, and many others.

What Is MC and How It Is Used?

MC simulation is named after the Monaco gambling spot. The MC technique was originally developed by Stanislaw Ulam, a mathematician who worked on the Manhattan project when recovering from brain surgery. The technique was developed in collaboration with John Von Neuman. Developers use MC simulation to model the probability of different outcomes such as identified risk occurrence. Usually, developers would use MC if the risk cannot be easily predicted. Usually, the difficulty with the prediction may be due to some intervening random variables.

Developers use the MC simulation technique to understand the impact of risk and uncertainty in a project risk prediction and forecasting model. The technique has been used in projects, science, engineering, and supply chains.

In a project risk analysis that has significant uncertainties, MC might be effective. Usually, in organizational projects, random variables may interfere with the risks, requiring the use of MC. MC tends to have an enormous array of variables that lend themselves to applications. It can be used, for example, to assess the probability of cost overruns in projects. The telecommunication industry has used MC to determine network performance to help optimize the network. The insurance industry and various industry silos have use MC when necessary.

Let's demonstrate how the MC technique can be used by projecting a price. Let's use historical price data from a historic asset:

periodic daily return = ln (day's price ÷ previous day's price)

Subsequently, we may use the AVERAGE, STDEV.P, and VAR.P functions on the whole resulting series to get the average daily return, standard deviation, and variance inputs, in this order. The next step is

drift = average daily return - (variance ÷ 2)

Instead, *drift* can be set to 0; this choice reflects a certain theoretical orientation, but the differences are not supposed to be far from each other, at least for shorter time frames.

Going forward, get a random input:

random value = standard deviation * NORMSINV(RAND())

The equation for the following day's price is:

next day's price = today's price * e ^ (drift + random value)

Now, use e to a given power x, and then use the EXP function: EXP(x). The calculation can be repeated the desired number of times (each repetition will represent one day) to obtain a simulation of future price movement. Generating a random number of simulations, it can assess the probability that a risk's price will follow a given trajectory.

Q-Learning

Q-learning is model-free reinforcement learning and goal to build the policy of the environment. Q provides the quality of action (A) for given state (S).

Bellman equation

$$v(s) = E[R_{t+1} + \lambda_v (S_{t+1})| S_t = s]$$

Where

E refers to expectation and

λ refers to discount factor; thus, the Q-value equation:

$$Q^\pi(s,a) = E[r_{t+1} + \lambda r_{t+2} + \lambda^2 r_{t+3} + ...| s,a]$$
$$= E_{s'}[r + \lambda Q^\pi(s',a')| s,a]$$

Optimum Q-value equation:

$$Q^*(s,a) = E_{s'}[r + \lambda \max_{a'} Q^*(s',a')| s,a]$$

Deep Q Network

The deep Q network is the extension of the Q-learning function to update the Q table, but with so many combinations to create these actions and states, to manage the rewards policy becomes complex, and it is impossible to manage many combinations created in the Q table. So, the deep

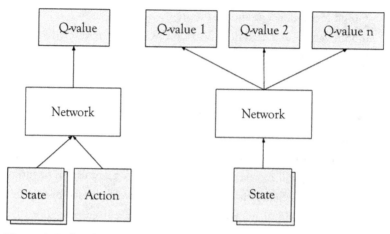

Figure 2.7 Q-value value network

Q network is the idea to create a neural network that will be approximate for each state and the different Q values for each action. See Figure 2.7. The logical sequence follows:

> State -> Deep Q Neural Network -> Q value Action 1, Q value Action 2 .. Q value Action n.

Deep reinforcement learning applications are used in the following areas:

- Games—Go, poker
- Robotics—Robot Controller
- Computer vision—recognition, detection
- NLP—language translation, conversational
- Finance—pricing, trading, risk management
- Systems—performance optimization

What Is Classification?

Classification is the problem that identifies a set of categories to which new observations belong. One of the most often used ML algorithms uses cases to classify certain differences to differentiate the category by classification.

Classification is the process of predicting the class of given data points. These classes are called targets or labels or categories. Classification modeling is the task of approximating a mapping function (f) from input variables (X) to discrete output variables (y).

So, Y = f(x)

A classification problem is when the output variable is a category, such as a "number" or "letter" or "disease" and "no disease." A classification model attempts to draw some conclusion from observed values. Given one or more inputs, a classification model will try to predict the value of one or more outcomes. The several classification models include logistic regression, decision tree, random forest, gradient-boosted tree, multilayer perceptron, one-vs-rest, and Naive Bayes.

Two types of learners in classification are lazy learners and eager learners. Lazy learners take less time to train and more time to predicting classification. Examples of lazy learners are k-nearest neighbor and case-based reasoning.

Eager learners construct a classification model based on the given training data and coverage to have the entire instance space. Eager learners take more time on training and less time on classifying. Examples of eager learnings are decision tree, Naive Bayes, and artificial neural networks.

Classification: Decision Tree Algorithm

Decision tree algorithm builds classification or regression models in the form of a tree structure with If–Then mutually exclusive rules and these rules learn sequentially using the training data. This process continues until it meets the termination condition. The problem with the decision tree is that it could easily get into the overfitting problem that means too many rules were constructed, limiting generalization.

CHAPTER 3

Introduction to Risk

- Definition of risk
- Risk examples: risk business case
- Different types of risks
- Risk management process
- Risk categories

Chapter Outline

- Define risk and provide examples
- Illustrate various risk areas
- Illustrate risk process areas in detail
- Determine risk mitigations
- Illustrate risk standards

Key Learning Points

- Learn and understand risk
- Identify risk areas
- Mitigate risk
- Understand what uncertainties exist
- Analyze and determine which events must have a planned response
- Adopt an approach for each risk event, defining what triggers a response
- Maintain risk plans
- Monitor risk occurrences

Definition of Risk

Risk can be defined as the possibility of gaining (good) or losing (bad) something such as financial benefits, time benefits, brand value, customer value, and any measurable value. Thus, two types of risks are positive and negative. While investing money into a business, financial gain is positive and financial loss is negative. Risk can be the uncertain potential, unpredictable, and uncontrollable outcome. Risk perception can be judgment people make about severity and possibility. Any task or action comes with some sort of risk.

Risk is uncertainty. Typical risk is facing an unfortunate situation, such as losing an investment. Another example is that an organization may have a lower than planned and budgeted trend of doing well in the financial calendar year.

Technical projects tend to be lean. This means challenges occur due to work with inadequate funding, staff, and equipment. To make matters worse, managers have a persistent expectation to complete projects faster than projected.

Some concerns lead to risk and include issues that are not addressed and allowed to persist in the corporate workspace. Some concerns may include:

- Issues that affect a project's time, schedule, cost, or quality and scope.
- Project or task areas that require assessment and executive review.
- Subsequent areas that do not address cultural or organizational changes, technical changes to applications, legal or contract changes, and the business/project sponsor owner with new requirements.

Occasionally people working on projects for corporations contribute people risks that consist of the following:

1. Late start of a project: At times, project personnel are unavailable at project start, perhaps due to finishing previous projects later than expected.

2. Occasionally, project resources may be lost due to resource resignation, promotion, reassignment, health, or other reasons.

3. Consultants and contract workers may be in short supply or unavailable. The firm may experience a temporary loss of staff due to illness, unusual busy work at the organization site, support priorities, or for other reasons.

4. Queuing could be an issue on projects due to slippage related to experts' commitment availability.

5. Lack of motivation can lead to a lack of team interconnection and interest; this is more likely to happen on long projects.

Other types of risks will be described in the examples provided.

Another example of a risk is that an organization may have a lower than planned and budgeted trend of doing well in the financial calendar year. Other related topics of risk will be explained in this chapter.

Example of a Risk Business Case

Risks in an organization/business sector can be dangerous and unpredictable for organizations. The following case studies are typical examples that provide clear examples.

Case Study 1: Blockbuster and Netflix

Purpose

The risk purpose for the Blockbuster and Netflix case illustrates how due diligence is important to commit to business dealings. Being too quick to get into an agreement can create problems for organizations. This means an investigation is required to look at positive and negative risks.

- Accountability of new trends and impact to large corporations and the risks associated.
- How do we avoid such new trend changes and impacts to other corporations?

- How do we detect business model trends early enough to save large corporations?
- Can we detect new trends to answer this problem?

Business Case Summary

The case study of Netflix (Reed Hastings, founder of Netflix) and Blockbuster (John Antioco, CEO of Blockbuster). In 2000, the founder of Netflix, based in Dallas, proposed a partnership to Blockbuster, which was atop the video rental industry. The proposal was that Netflix could run Blockbuster's brand online and Blockbuster could promote Netflix in its stores. Eventually Blockbuster went bankrupt in 2010 and Netflix became $28 billion company.

Hastings is widely hailed as a genius and Antioco is considered a fool. Scientists for the past 15 years studied the incident and now they know how the networks function and how this incident could have been avoided.

The lesson of risk stems from the notion that in 2000, Blockbuster had thousands of retail locations and millions of customers with enormous budgets and efficient operations that dominated the competition in this business sector. Unfortunately, Blockbuster had a weakness of charging its customers for late fees. This was an important model that earned them enormous revenue. Netflix did not have the same late fees and did not have locations. Customers could watch videos if they wanted or return them to get another one. However, customer needed to have a subscription to rent videos. This worked well for Netflix. The lesson here was that a risky business model led to the downfall of the Blockbuster corporation.

This is one example of business model risk: Blockbuster did not incorporate a new type of business model and new technological trends. Positive risk was the Netflix approach and negative risk was that Blockbuster had fallen into a trap. Similarly, AI is heading into new technological trends and industrial revolutionary business model transformations. Corporations should embrace this model trend sooner than later to avoid business model risk, making a positive risk by using the opportunity.

Case Study 2: Taxi Business and Uber

Purpose

The purpose of the Taxi and Uber case illustrates how due diligence is important when starting a business without thorough research, and what is to come. Too eager to adopt a business model and commit fully can hurt the growth and prospects of the organization. This means an investigation is required to consider the positive and negative risks associated with such business models.

- Consideration and due diligence of the corporation and the associated risks.
- How do we incorporate research and expected changes to clients' needs to reflect the business model?
- How do we detect possible risks in the business model?

Business Case Summary

The regular taxi business has been straightforward, answering the need if a person needed a ride from Point A to Point B. They would just call the taxi office and specify the goal location. The taxi specifies the amount to pay or lets the meter in the vehicle tally the distance and amount. Some taxis can be stopped on the road and told the destination. The taxi driver specifies the amount to be paid, and once at the destination, the customer pays the driver the agreed amount. Here are additional advantages for Uber:

1. A driver can drive their vehicles based on prior arrangement with Uber bookings.
2. Log into your phone app and drop customers at specified locations.
3. Uber driving is not a full-time business.
4. A driver makes money and customer fees are lower.
5. Customers can call from anywhere. This is convenient for the customer.
6. Uber created a business model transformation.

The conventional taxi business model has been lucrative everywhere in the United States until recently. Uber Technologies Inc., doing business as Uber, introduced taxi service with a new business model. The Uber taxi business model operates differently. The customer can book Uber car service by using an application on the customer's cell phone. The service is relatively safe because of controls built into the application and the services it offers. The driver of the Uber car is checked to make sure they have no security issues. The customer knowing that Uber drivers are relatively safe attracts more customers to use the service. Uber drivers use their vehicles to operate under the Uber business name. The service is attractive and has taken some business from the conventional taxi service.

Regular taxi drivers have felt the pinch of losing business to Uber. The effect is that taxi drivers have lost income (KATZ March 28, 2018) leading to suicide among some taxi drivers. On March 16, 2018, Nicanor Ochisor, a 65-year-old yellow cab driver, took his own life in his New York Queens home. His family reported he has been worrying about losing revenue. Nicanor paid a great deal of money to obtain his taxi medallion and was not making adequate money to enable him to retire. In February 2018, a similar case happened to taxi driver Douglas Schifter. Douglas shot himself outside City Hall after posting a long statement on Facebook blaming politicians for saturating the streets with taxi cabs that included Uber taxis. The New York Taxi Workers Alliance, a nonprofit group that advocates for drivers, reported that two other incidents of drivers killing themselves occurred due to financial pressures.

Case Study 3: Enron Case Study

Purpose

The purpose of the Enron case illustrates how financial accountability in an organization is important in leading to growth or collapse of an organization without thorough research and what is to come (Segal 2018). Not auditing and ensuring accountability may lead to risk problems. This means companies should adopt an appropriate risk standard.

- Accountability of financial declarations of the corporation to stakeholders and the risks associated.
- How do we avoid such incidents happening to other corporations?
- How do we detect such incidents early?

Business Case Summary

In 2001, a U.S. corporation, Enron, based in Houston, Texas, ran into accountability problems with the law due to lies in the organization's merger between Houston Natural Gas and InterNorth. Both organizations are small regional companies. Enron employed about 20,000 employees and was named one of the Fortune innovative companies for six consecutive years.

By 2001, it was found that Enron reported financial information that turned out to be institutional, systematic, and creatively planned fraud, later known as the Enron scandal. This led to corporation accounting practices and activities in the United States and subsequently led to the enactment of the Sarbanes–Oxley Act of 2002. This enactment affected the greater business world by causing a dissolution of Arthur Andersen, an accounting firm. Enron eventually filed for bankruptcy in the Southern District of New York in late 2001, using Weil, Gotshal & Manges as its bankruptcy counsel. Enron eventually sold its last remaining business, Prisma Energy International Incorporation on September 7, 2006, to Ashmore Energy International Ltd. (currently called AEI).

The idea is to investigate the truth about the claims that enabled them to be innovative six times. Was Enron truthful and ethical in their business dealings?

The intended audience of the corporation is project stakeholders such as the business owner and senior leadership.

Business Need

Were there risk violations that made Enron look good for nominating six times? It is important that similar incidents be analyzed and have immediate resolutions.

Goals/Scope

A similar incident may likely happen in the short term or over time. It is important corporations and merger organizations identify such occurrences and quickly stop unethical occurrences.

Risks/Issues

Organizations need to check if there are risk areas that include schedule, initial costs, life-cycle costs, technical obsolescence, feasibility, reliability of systems, dependencies/interoperability, surety considerations, future procurements, project management, overall project failure, organizational/change management, business, data/information, technology, strategic, security, privacy, project resources, and project lies.

Everyone lies (Cothenet 2016). Lies may cause damage through investigation, and organizations should carry out investigation and ensure accountability.

High-Level Business Impact

Any damaging operations are likely to create false assumptions that can tarnish the reputation of a corporation. Here are some reputation issues that can damage an organization:

1. Legal issues
2. Loss of reputation
3. Loss of finance/revenue
4. Employees may lose their jobs
5. Companies may go out of business
6. Loss to investors

Alternatives and Analysis

Analysis

How could this have been avoided?

How can we determine a reputable auditing firm for the corporation?

How can we confirm that the corporation is conforming to government regulations and policies?

Is this too good to be true?

Is it statistically verifiable?

Is the data collected projected or actual data?

Alternative A

Check this organization frequently for ethical accountability. The budget should be reviewed as a top priority. Who audited the account, and can this person be trusted to do a thorough job consistently? Check if the generation of the budget is too blurred or if the budget is insufficient. If it is insufficient, ask the stakeholders to explain the situation and ask them to revise the budget or change the scope of the project or entities used to conclude the budget.

Alternative B

If an unethical finding emerges, legal action will be used against the firm.

Preferred Solution

Financial Considerations:

- Financial accountability should be well detailed. This will include assumptions and supporting documents.
- What data need to be collected to justify appropriate accountability?
- Which data points need to be collected and statistically verified?

Uncertainties on any of the task area should focus on risk and risk management. This means care and attention should be taken to plan risk and risk management well. Let's spend some time discussing how risk should be managed.

Different Types of Risks

Natural Risks

Natural risk can be categorized as earth processes. Typical examples of natural risks are flooding, hurricanes, tornadoes, earthquakes, volcanic eruptions, tsunamis, and other geologic occurrences. Natural disasters can cause death, can damage property, and typically leaves some economic damage in its wake. Further causes of severe damage depends on the affected population settings. Infrastructure can be damaged severely.

Country-Specific Risks

Country risks relate to the borders of a country and focus on related financial commitments. Risk may extend to political and economic unrest of the country. Business in a country may experience risk that must be considered. A typical example of country risk is purchasing a bond in countries such as Canada and Mexico. One of those countries may end up defaulting. The assessment will depend on the stability of the countries. One can assume that the default is more likely to happen in Mexico, because of the tax systems in the countries. The analysis will depend on the evidence of corruption in the countries, inflation rates, demographics, and education. Other factors may also lead to the prediction of risk. Further analysis will show that Mexico's initial purchase is less than that of Canada. However, purchasing the bond in Mexico will likely cost less.

To evaluate country risk, analysts must consider qualitative and quantitative analysis.

An effective way to diversify stock is through international investing, but countries in which to invest must be chosen carefully. Deciding to invest in Mexico and Italy is not the same as investing in the United States. The careful analyst will consider the country's economic and political risks that affect its businesses and affects investment losses.

Industry-Specific Risks

Investors may face various risks in industrial silos. Examples are provided in the following.

Industry-specific risk can be categorized into different industries such as construction (i.e., construction falls, quality controls, and managing construction defects), retail (i.e., product recall, managing crowds, and parking lot safety), and restaurants (i.e., kitchen safety, foodborne illness, kitchen staff cuts, and burns). Various industries face specific risks that may occur in another industry or are unique to that industry. Risks may align with daily activities, the equipment being used, or simply the type of business. Retail businesses have different types of risk from restaurant businesses. Further, resources can be used to address and minimize risk, and to promote safety in industries. Analysts should make efforts to minimize workplace accidents or injuries. Also, costs should be controlled appropriately.

Some risks can be controlled, such as investing in stocks. Although risky, the risk can be controlled with appropriate care and discipline. Here, thoughtful selection of investment to answer individual goals will keep individual stock and bond risks at an acceptable threshold.

Functional Area Risks

Functional area risks are typically referenced in areas such as division management, facility management, and security. These risks include allocation of building perimeters, chemical storage, elevators, entrances and exits, information security, parking areas, roof openings, shipping and receiving, warehouses, windows, and additional areas.

Departmental Risks

Numerous risks can affect departments in completing project objectives. We list a few risks:

Accidental hazards, acts of nature, client-related risk, employee risk, environmental risk, financial risk, fraud/corruption, hostile actions from others, landlord-related risk, legal risk, partner or supplier/contractor risk, political risk, process risk, public-opinion risk, and technology risk.

Subject Matter Risks

Subject matter risk is relevant to the following risk areas:

- Country risk (i.e., political, environment, security, etc.).
- Business risk (i.e., customer capability to pay, creditworthiness, market factors, etc.).
- Contract risk (i.e., liability, price, type, penalties, etc.).
- Project risk (i.e., resources, skill set, methodology, product stability, etc.).
- Technology risk (i.e., solution, architecture, hardware and software infrastructure network, delivery channels, etc.).

Corporate Risk

Corporate risk is common in corporations. This is a broad range of risk to clients ranging from small business sectors to multinational corporations. Corporate risk requires management that will minimize financial losses. Risk management relates to external threats to a corporation such as fluctuations in the financial market that affect the corporation's financial assets.

Here are examples of typical corporate risks:

- Information technology risk (i.e., issues include data integrity, data leakage, loss of intellectual property, or cybercrime).
- Fraud (i.e., employee misconduct may arise in a difficult economic climate).
- Cost reduction pressure (i.e., a significant portion of the increase in profits may have to be achieved through cost reductions).
- Increased competitive pressure in the organization (i.e., consumer spending has dropped to new lows; executives need to innovate products, prioritize customer service, reduce expenses on current offerings, and expand their product portfolio).
- Compliance (i.e., expect more intense scrutiny and regulation of business practices).
- Liquidity risk (i.e., bank credit availability remains limited and companies may need to explore alternative funding sources).

- Talent risk (i.e., the market for talented and skilled professionals is flourishing and may lead to retaining and engaging employees as a human resource issue).
- Political trends (i.e., economic discontent or expanding universal geopolitical risk).
- The high cost of capital (i.e., credit crises and a high cost of capital are likely to persist until global credit markets stabilize).
- Strategic change management (i.e., business transformations such as mergers, divestitures, and internal organizations).

Start-Up Risks

Every start-up business encounters some sort of risk. Typical start-up risks range from ideation to ongoing development:

- Trusting a key employee
- Relying on cash flow
- Abandoning the steady paycheck
- Sacrificing personal capital
- Estimating popular interest
- Betting on a crucial deadline
- Investing personal time, funds, and health

All seven listed items can create an enormous risk for the start-up organization.

Security Risks

Security issues are everywhere. Two forces can cause risk:

- Enemies are getting better and faster at making their threats stick.
- Companies that still struggle with an overload in urgent security tasks.

Here is a collection of IT security risks that need to be noted for organizations to consider:

- Failure to cover cybersecurity basics.
- Not understanding what generates corporate cybersecurity risks.
- Lack of a cybersecurity policy.
- Confusing compliance with cybersecurity.
- The human factor plays an important role in how strong (or weak) the organization's information security defenses are. Lower level employees can weaken security considerations. Organizations must watch the security setup and monitor access levels.
- Bring-your-own-device policy and the cloud. One in five organizations suffered a mobile security breach.
- Funding, talent, and resource constraints can lead to enormous problems in an organization.
- Little or no information security training for stakeholders.
- Lack of a recovery plan.
- Constantly evolving risks: polymorphic malware risks (type of malware that constantly changes its identifiable features to evade detection) are harmful and destructive, or intrusive computer software such as a virus, worm, trojan, or spyware.

Risk Management Process

We describe the risk management overview in detail, including the following processes (Heldman, July 5, 1905). This approach follows the PMI PMBOK Standards. The standard processes are plan risk management, identify risks, perform qualitative risk analysis, perform quantitative risk analysis, plan risk responses, implement risk responses, and monitor risks.

The processes are manually based and AI solutions for risk are redefined using an approach applying AI in a generalized fashion.

See Figure 3.1 for the generalized risk approach. Also see the Risk Management Overview Table 3.1 PMBOK 6 (PMI 2017).

The Project Risk Management Plan is a high-level plan that details other risk processes. The resources working on the project determine the effort that will be put into taking care of the likelihood of the risk that

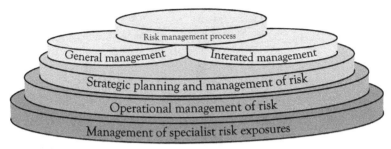

Figure 3.1 Risk management process

will occur. The following entities go into project risk management: scope, schedule, and budget are the primary areas of project risk that information going into project risk management must address clearly and well.

The collected risk data will be used to analyze the AI system. Tables will be created from the risk management processes that can be used in the AI system.

This plan becomes a component of the Project Management Plan, documenting how the remaining risk processes will be performed.

Plan risk management with data that can be analyzed using Table 3.1, indicating the structure of each risk process. The process for each risk will be defined in detail. First, let us define what process means here.

Table 3.1 Risk management process

Process	Purpose
Plan Risk Management	Overall planning of the risk that may occur. This process enables planning risk management activities aiming to increase positive risk and minimize negative risk.
	Plan risk management defines how risks associated with the project will be identified, analyzed, and managed. In this section, we outline how risk management activities are performed, recorded, and monitored throughout the life cycle of the project and describe, at a high level, the process to be used to record and prioritize risks by the risk manager or risk management team.
Identify Risks	Determine ways to identify risks. The process documents individual risks and their sources, subsequently helping the project team respond to the identified risks appropriately.
Perform Qualitative Risk Analysis	The process of prioritizing individual risks for further analysis or actions on their priorities using the probability of occurrence and impact focused on high priority risks. This process is repeated over the life of the project.

Perform Quantitative Risk Analysis	Numerically analyzing individual risks with other sources of uncertainties combined with overall impact. Literally, it quantifies overall risks exposure on the project. Additionally, it provides quantitative risk information that helps with risk planning responses. It is important that the process is carried out after qualitative analysis is performed. The process is completed through the project life cycle, as needed.
Plan Risk Responses	This process enables developing options, selecting appropriate strategies and actions, and treating individual risks. Responses enable resources to be allocated and document risk details. This process is repeated throughout the project life cycle.
Implement Risk Responses	Developing options and strategies for the identified risk as agreed in the plan. Agreed responses are implemented as planned to address the identified risk. This process is repeated throughout the project life cycle.
Monitor Risks	Watching for possible signs of risk and taking appropriate action to mitigate or remove it. This process enables the decision to be based on currently identified risks.

Developing a Process

Processes make up the Process Management Institute project management approach. A process consists of three parts: input, tools and techniques, and output. This approach is adopted in this book (see Table 3.2).

Input is the initial information required to start the process, such as the company's background information, procedures, and requirements before the project starts. The tools and techniques are the experiences, other procedures, and tools required to use the inputs to generate the output. The output varies based on the input, tools and techniques, and requirements of the project. The following icons will be used to denote the requirement.

To create a process, appropriate internal documents are inputs from the organization or outside the organization. The inputs are used by the tools and techniques to get one or more output. A general scenario is putting an orange into a blender and getting orange juice at the end. The orange is the input to the blender. The blender is the tool, and the technique is the expertise of the person using the blender to produce the orange juice. The orange juice is the output. See Figure 3.2: Project Process Diagram.

Table 3.2 Process Icons

OUTPUT	Initial information required to create process output. This will be provided by other processes or documents created during the overall process.
Tools and Techniques	Tools and techniques are the actions taken to create output. Several tools, methods, or techniques can be used in different processes and provide specific information or operations to achieve the objectives of the process. In general, a tool or technique consists of the following examples. The acronym STAMPED is useful when preparing for certification S: Systems, Skills, Software T: Templates A: Analysis, Audits M: Methods, Meetings (including reviews, training, team building, negotiations, bidder conference) P: Performance Measurements E: EVM (Earn Value Management), Expert Judgment D: Decomposition, Diagramming
	Results are created or generated using input and tools and techniques. The results can be of two types. First, the creation of a new document or action that will affect other processes; second, the output may directly affect other actions or processes.

Each process identified in the process table is described in terms of the aforementioned model or methodology. For each input, several sources are provided. They could be previous documents or information obtained in a previous process. For example, the Project Charter is one of the very first documents created when a project is to be initiated. This document and all its relevant information are used to guide other processes. Also, see Figure 3.2.

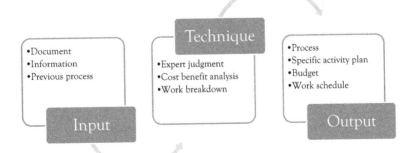

Figure 3.2 Project process diagram

Input and Output Process

For example, in the *Tools and Techniques for Define Activities*, as shown as follows, we described the concept of decomposition, templates, and expert judgment earlier in the chapter. Next, we describe the new item, *Rolling Wave Planning*.

Example	Decomposition
	Rolling Wave Planning
	Templates
	Expert Judgment

The output process has two possible effects. The first effect is that the process may create a new document, new information, or new processes. The second is that the output can affect existing processes or documents. We summarize the input and output processes for that area, providing a data-flow diagram to demonstrate how the information connects to the project. It is helpful to use the rolling wave planning approach to consider each piece of the project related to risk.

Risk management consists of planning, identification, analysis, response planning, response implementation, and monitoring risk on the project. The objectives of project management are to increase the possibilities of positive risk and to decrease the impact of negative risks.

Points: Case Story of Blockbuster and Netflix

Example of business model risk: Blockbuster did not adhere to the new technological trend (Newman September 23, 2010). AI could have been applied for a solution. The new technology trend builds on social media and one can watch this approach. Here is a typical trend that needs to be watched:

- Taxi business and Uber: New technological trend, better pricing model, and ease of driver sign on.
- Enron business burst, use Enron case study.
- Use other three business cases as applicable as possible.

Risk can occur based on lies on the project, as in the case study of Enron Purpose of

- Accountability of financial declaration of a corporation to stakeholders and the risks associated.
- How do we avoid such incidents happening to other corporations?
- How do we detect such incidents early?

Business Case Summary

The following business case issues need to be mitigated, and the approach is provided next.

Positive Risk (Opportunities) Response Strategies

One can engage strategic responses to positive and negative risks. Let us look at each of the strategies.

The list of identified risks is recorded in the Risk Register. A Risk Register is an artifact generally used in risk management and project management. The purpose is to help assure regulatory compliance and stay current with potential issues that can derail intended outcomes. Identified risks are categorized into positive and negative strategies that need to be used appropriately.

Strategies use specific information regarding category, priority, urgency, schedule, and budget impact values. The probability of each occurring is described as follows.

Exploit

This response strategy is used to ensure that the risk happens to get the perceived benefit from the situation. Simple ways to do this could be to train the team to give them extra skills or to adjust the deliverables slightly so they respond better to the opportunity.

Share

A good aspect of the share response is in bidding for work or procurement. It is successful if the project bid involves being partnered or sharing with another firm. The opportunity of winning the bid would be more likely to happen if working as a team.

Enhance

Enhancing the opportunity can come about when focused on the causes of the opportunity. In this strategy, it will be appropriate to focus on factors that are going to make this positive risk/opportunity happen. An example is by introducing software features to make the new product more marketable or shareable.

Accept

The accept strategy is used simply to accept the risk of the opportunity coming to the corporation. If nothing is done to influence the opportunity, then it could have a negative effect instead.

Negative Risks (Threats) Response Strategies

Negative risk strategies are useful for identified risks and may hurt the project. Using these strategies will help mitigate identified risks.

Mitigate

A mitigation strategy lessens the impact of the risk by trying to decrease either the probability of the risk happening or the impact of the risk. This strategy tends to decrease the severity of the risk.

Transfer

In the transfer risk response strategy, the idea is to transfer the risk to a third party to manage. Transferring does not eliminate the risk; rather, it only transfers the responsibility of managing the risk to the third party. Vehicle insurance is a typical example.

Avoid

Avoidance is a desired risk response strategy mainly used for critical risks and is the best technique for almost all risks. It cannot be used most of the time. It is easy to use this strategy if the risk is identified in the very early stage; otherwise, it is difficult to adopt this strategy because in a later stage, changing scope or schedule is a costly affair.

Accept

The acceptance risk response strategy is used for positive and negative risks. No action is needed to manage the risk except acknowledging it. Project managers use this strategy when the risk is not critical or if a response is not reasonable, based on the importance of the risk.

General Risks

Brief Qualitative and Quantitative Risk Analysis Summary

The qualitative analysis starts by determining whether the risk event requires a response. Risks that are thought to be significant will be analyzed further using risk quantification. Risks that are considered limited in impact and probability may be documented and put in lower rankings as a result of qualitative analysis. In all cases, no risk is left alone without being documented in the Risk Register. It is important that each identified risk is fully understood. The risks that are not understood may require further analysis that may lead to quantitative analysis. Quantitative risk analysis can take time and be expensive, stretching the project budget. At times, risk can be overemphasized, which takes up time and resources that should have been allocated to more worthy events. Often overemphasis happens when incorporating project management. If the project team did not previously realize the risk, and directed all efforts to other prioritized tasks until the team ran into difficulties moving forward, project management is not paying attention to critical areas of the project. The team needs to mitigate the risk very quickly, before the project fails.

Probability and impact are essential for analyzing and prioritizing risks. Determining the probability of risk-taking carries consequences. A scale is used to quantify the risks. The risks are quantified using the same measure and are prioritized accordingly.

Risk ranking enables comparability among projects. This analysis helps the project team and management understand the project's pending risks. Here, the team can decide whether they should continue or terminate the project, if the risk is outside their risk tolerance level or threshold. Costs, schedules, and other planning become more realistic based on risk analysis. Going forward, the investigation may be needed for the top ranking risks to identify factors that may have been considered.

What Is Risk Categorization?

Risk is an important component of tasks or projects undertaken daily. It is important to categorize risks because they are part of daily life. However, risks in corporate settings may come in many forms ranging from financial loss to losing important business transactions to a competitor or loss of reputation. Based on experience, some risks are accidental and unanticipated. Some risks can be anticipated and planned for using standards such as the Project Management Institute guidelines for managing risk. To help identify risk easily, it is necessary to group risks, which can be beneficial in several ways:

- Making effort to avoid surprising situations.
- Providing a structured, focused approach to identifying problems.
- Developing more effective risk mitigation techniques.
- Applying better strategies for responding to risks.
- Enhancing organizational communication by including employees.
- Making a conscious effort to monitor risk using various simplified risk approaches.

One approach is to use common frameworks of risks to refine them to suit an organization environment's unique situation. A typical example appears in the following.

Risk Response

Let us consider identified risks, put them categories, and determine possible mitigations.

Common Root Causes of Project Risks

1. Inappropriate or poor leadership at any level. The project manager, acting as a leader, needs management to help as well to ensure project success. The project manager and management need to collaborate.

2. Ethical misalignment and incorrect culture. If ethical misalignment and inappropriate culture are entertained in the project environment, disorientation on the project may result and team members may not have the motivation to perform sufficiently well for the project to be successful.

3. It is quite worthwhile to plan well and use appropriate planning processes. If a project is planned well, the project will have a great chance of being successful. Planning well incorporates functional and nonfunctional requirements including short-term tasks.

4. It is practical and efficient to document progress on a project. This approach helps ensure that important points are not overlooked. Documenting the project progress will help determine which areas need resources to complete the project in a timely manner.

5. Based on appropriate planning, the project team can set expectations and manage them progressively. The project team needs to be managed using hard and soft management techniques. If this approach and technique are not used properly, clearly defined consequences will ensue that are bad for the project. Planning leads to prioritized tasks that are appropriately assigned to competent stakeholders.

6. Stakeholders must be well trained to carry out project work efficiently. The project manager needs to be well trained and capable of carrying out the project successfully. Management responsibilities must be assigned to individuals who have the capabilities to meet requirements. If the manager is poorly trained, the project may fail.

7. The project budget must be calculated accurately. If the budget is not estimated well it can lead to problems. Improper calculation may cause the cost of an undertaking to be underestimated. Once the project runs out of resources, it is difficult to complete it successfully. This approach requires identifying a lack of resources early in the life of the project.

8. Communication is one of the most important entities in project management. If communication is not carried out correctly, complications can result. Communications should be done appropriately among management executives, the project manager, and team members. It is important that stakeholders feel free to share their concerns or suggestions.

9. It is important to ensure competing resources are not stretched in manpower and financing. Good cost estimates avoid problems.

10. It is important to pay attention to risks that show up on the project. If the warning signs are ignored, project problems may result and add up quickly.

Risk Categories

We list the various risk categories to provide brief knowledge here. We discussed the risk categories in earlier parts of the book.

Identification of Similarities

The system is capable of identifying similar risk issues that can be used to provide solutions, perhaps requiring an artificial neural network to be

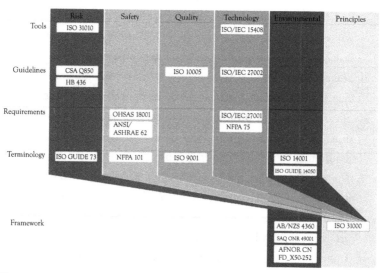

Figure 3.3 Risk management ISO classification.

used. The AI engine being used has neural networks built in. The system's ability to learn from current data is based on the use of neural networks.

AI and the building blocks of the knowledge base connect.

Risk Management Standard

International Organization for Standardization (ISO) 31000:2018, Risk management guidelines provide principles, a framework, and a process for managing risk. Any organization can use the risk management guidelines regardless of its size, activity, or sector. https://iso.org/iso-31000-risk-management.html (see Figure 3.3).

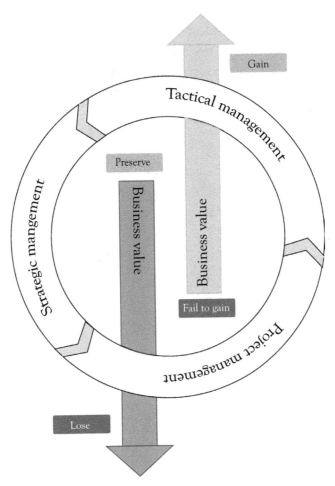

Figure 3.4 ISO 31000 business value

The ISO, based in Geneva, is represented by 163 member countries in the world. It has published over 19,000 international standards that can be viewed at www.iso.org. Here are some of the standards: ISO Guide 73: 2009 focusing on risk management and vocabulary. ISO 31000-2013 on risk management provides guidance for the implementation of ISO31000. ISO31004, based on risk management, provides guidance on the implementation of ISO31000 ISO31010:21009 on risk management. Risk assessment techniques provide how to implement ISO 31000 in an organization. ISO 31010: 2009 on risk management and assessment techniques guides companies on how to select and apply systematic techniques for risk assessment. ISO 31000 guides the selection and application of techniques to assess risk in a wide range of situations, assisting firms in making decisions where there is uncertainty. The goal is to provide information about risks as part of a process for managing risk. The standard provides summaries of a range of techniques, with references to other documents where the techniques are described in greater detail. The current version of the standard provides more details on the process of planning, implementing, verifying, and validating the use of the techniques.

See Figure 3.4 for risk standards. The figure illustrates strategic management, tactical management, and project management. These three encompass business value in terms of preserve and fail/gain.

CHAPTER 4

Knowledge Base

Chapter Outline

- Define the knowledge base for the AI project
- Risk knowledge development
- Objectives of the risk knowledge base
- Identification of knowledge for risk
- Knowledge acquisition for risk
- Knowledge sharing

Key Learning Points

- Learn and understand the knowledge base
- Understand risk knowledge base development

Artificial intelligence (AI) can be used repeatedly in applications with different needs. Human resources departments in corporations have had difficulties capturing and using the human intelligence required in organizations. Knowledge and intelligence must be captured and used repeatedly. The captured knowledge and intelligence can be stored in the knowledge base, used to build a knowledge model, and train machines, so it can be used when necessary.

To capture and use human intelligence requires the development of an integrated information system. The idea is to develop an integrated system that can supply all the knowledge required by human experts. These integrated systems should be readily available and shareable. The integrated system should be used with strategic objectives in mind, leading to the development of AI.

Companies use AI to solve important challenges based on the information stored in the knowledgebase. As observed in life and business, human experts have cyclical demands. Similar approaches are applied to risk management that can be explored with use cases.

It is planned that the knowledgebase stores data, techniques, and algorithms that will be used to drive the AI integrated system. The integrated system will be introduced gradually in this approach. The objective of the AI integrated system is to focus on seeking mitigation solutions to risk in corporate settings. The objectives cause AI to consider using business rules that consists of "what if" questions. The AI considered strategic rules and logic to determine possible strategic mitigation solutions to using the data stored in the knowledgebase. The AI integrated system impacts knowledge objectives, identification of knowledge, knowledge acquisition, knowledge development, knowledge sharing, preservation of knowledge, fixing of knowledge, use of knowledge, evaluation of knowledge, measurement of knowledge, integration of the AI case-based knowledge representation of risk cases, identification of similarities, and connection of AI. All of these aspects are the building blocks of the knowledge base. Bizstats.ai is fundamentally built from inception to full-blown AI integrated systems using the knowledgebase.

Risk Knowledge Development

The purpose of this section is to generate the risk knowledge required, including ideas, models, skills, processes, and methods to train and learn. Machine-based learning has potential in various forms. With machine learning (ML), neural networks—pattern-based learning—will be used, enabling appropriate knowledge from a large amount of risk data, in turn enabling change of behavior of the captured data in the AI system.

Objectives of the Risk Knowledge Base

The level of skills and knowledge will be developed to use appropriate corporate objectives in the Bizstats.ai risk knowledgebase.

The objectives of risk in the knowledgebase follow:

- To capture associated risks from the data, process, people, things (e.g., IoT), systems, and actions.

- To determine occurrence.
- To determine impact of risks.
- To determine risk priority.
- To allocate risk owner.
- To determine risk mitigation.
- To determine risk action.
- To monitor risk continuously in real time and determine corrective actions.

Identification of Knowledge for Risk

The corporate setting will be used to model skills and knowledge that is appropriate to enable the AI to work well. This process requires mapping the collected risk knowledge. Every effort will be made to store the data in a form that will enable the data to be retrieved correctly. This AI system will allow access to collected data. Ultimately, the system should be able to build a corporate knowledge base capable of being extended with new risk data. The AI system will have the ability to prevent any loss of information, retain, and ensure all of the risk data up to date. The system will automatically be capable of building the knowledgebase. Subsequently, AI will be able to search for additional information externally.

Knowledge Acquisition for Risk

Risk data will be collected using formal and informal channels. The data will be used internally and externally. The collected data will enable suitable competencies of the AI system. The data will ultimately come from experts and will be used with statistical, ML algorithms.

Knowledge Sharing

Risk knowledge sharing is a critical part of the knowledge management cycle. It is important to realize that people, technology, and the corporate world are part of this phase. With AI knowledge sharing solutions, machine intelligence is capable of learning from other AI systems through real-time connectivity using real-time API. Discovering trends in a specific area, such as risk mitigation, can be effective. Another area where AI has been used efficiently is in the manufacture of vehicles. Humans have no need to go through the repetitive task of using the data. The computer system does the job efficiently without being overwhelmed. Bizstats.ai has real-time API access to solve knowledge sharing problems.

CHAPTER 5

AI Solutions for Risk

- Definition of AI solutions or risk
- Project plan
  o Define the business case
  o Current state of risk
  o Proposed goal state
- Going into AI/ML in-depth
- Proposed AI/ML risk processes
  o Identify risk or threat model
  o Risk categorization/classification model
  o Predicting risk-impact model
  o Risk-probability occurrence model
  o Risk priority model
  o Root cause analytics/analysis
  o Risk mitigation strategy recommendation
  o Risk-contingency recommendation
  o Risk monitoring and corrective action

Chapter Outline

- How to handle the AI/ML model for risk problems?

Key Learning Points

- Learn and understand how AI/ML applies to risk areas
- Data preparation for
  o Input
  o Output
  o Training data
  o Validation data
- Evaluate different algorithms

Purpose

To create machine learning (ML)/artificial intelligence (AI) solutions to risk management.

Background

An organization will face many risk issues that need to be resolved in a timely manner. Risk is becoming a bigger problem because of the large volume of data, the variety of risks, and challenges on new types of risk. To resolve risk manually takes a long time and large teams; thus, ML/AI solutions will be helpful to risk analysts.

- Problem statement
- Identify the risk or threat model
- Risk categorization/classification model
- Predicting the risk-impact model
- Risk-probability occurrence model
- Risk priority model
- Root cause analytics/analysis
- Risk mitigation strategy recommendation
- Risk-contingency recommendation
- Conclusion

First let us define a project plan. Here is the project plan.

Define the Project Plan

Background

Develop an AI system that can be referenced in the AI and Risk Book. Developing the AI system will provide proof of concept and proof of value over the traditional approach of a manually applied risk process. So far, no standard AI mitigation system can handle risk issues. Many innovative devices include Internet of Things, robotics, and sensors.

Goals

- Show that ideas mentioned in the book work.
- Show that using AI algorithms are useful and work.
- Select appropriate algorithms that can yield correct results.
- Show that similar AI systems can be developed using appropriate algorithms.

Scope

Design and build an AI system that will gear toward mitigation for risk. The AI will not consider areas that do not have anything to do with risk mitigation.

Key Stakeholders

Potential readers	Corporation resources
Absolut-e	Resources
Project manager	Archie
Project team members	Muthu, Venkat, Srini, additional Absolut-e Resources

Project Milestones

- Define AI system requirements
- High-level AI design
- Detail AI design
- Research
- Data collection
- Proof of value and proof concept write-ups (outputs)

Project Budget

Absolut-e Data com Inc will absorb the project budget expenses.

Risk

Constraints, Assumptions, Risks, and Dependencies

Constraints	Absolut-e is developing the AI system, but would not show every detailed part of the system. However, it would ensure the system works well.
Assumptions	The system will work well, considering risk requirements. Business cases will be used for the development of the AI system.
Risks and dependencies	The system may not work as required. The system will depend on appropriate specified requirements and subsequent design. If appropriate data are not collected correctly, the outcome of the system could give false results.

Define Business Case

A corporation wants to create a new innovative product.

Purpose

To yield an AI system for risk mitigation based on the corporation's point of view.

Current State of Risk Process

Now, it is necessary to ensure that possible risks are identified to save time and money.

Initially, the team needs to meet to develop the necessary risks to ensure the risks are annotated properly and accurately. A Risk Register will be used as one of the main artifacts.

Proposed Goal State Process

Here are the AI/ML models proposed to be in the goal state of the risk process:

1. Identify the risk or threat model.
2. Risk categorization/classification model.
3. Predict the risk-impact model.
4. Risk-probability-occurrence model.
5. Risk priority model.
6. Root cause analytics/analysis—not covered in this book.
7. Risk mitigation strategy recommendation—not covered in this book.

Figure 5.1 ML/AI risk process

8. Risk-contingency recommendation—not covered in this book.
9. Risk monitoring and corrective action—not covered in this book (see Figure 5.1).

AI/ML Risk Processes

Let us go over each of the proposed AI/ML risk processes with high-level steps.

1. Identify the risk or threat model:

- Define the goal of the ML/AI model for risk identification.
- Collect risk data.
- Design an algorithm for the threat model.
- Train the threat model.
- Test the threat model.

- Evaluate the threat model.
- Publish/produce the threat model.

2. Risk categorization/classification model:

- Define the goal of the model for risk categorization.
- Collect the risk category and risk data.
- Select and use the classification algorithm.
- Train the classification model.
- Test the classification model.
- Evaluate the classification model.
- Publish/produce the classification model.

3. Predicting the risk-impact model:

- Define the goal of the model for predicting risk impact.
- Collect risk-impact data from historical occurrences or from an expert.
- Design an algorithm to predict the risk-impact model.
- Train the risk-impact model.
- Test the risk-impact model.
- Evaluate the risk-impact model.
- Publish/produce the risk-impact model.

4. Risk-probability occurrence model:

- Define the goal of the model for risk-probability impact.
- Collect risk-probability data from historical occurrences or from an expert.
- Design an algorithm for the prediction of risk-probability occurrence.
- Train the risk-probability-occurrence model.
- Test the risk-probability-occurrence model.
- Evaluate the risk-probability-occurrence model.
- Publish/produce the risk-probability-occurrence model.

5. Risk priority model:

- Define the goal of the model for risk priority.
- Calculate data for risk priority.
- Design an algorithm for the prediction of the risk priority model.
- Train the risk priority model.
- Test the risk priority model.
- Evaluate the risk priority model.
- Publish/produce the risk priority model.

6. Root cause analytics/analysis:

- Determine the root cause of the identified risk and the analytics/analysis that will be used.

7. Risk mitigation strategy recommendation:

- Determine risk mitigation recommendations that may be used, based on the identified risk.
- Risk-contingency recommendation.
- Determine the risk-contingency recommendation that will be used, based on the risk type and category.

Risk Process Life Cycle

The risk process life cycle follows processes in the current environment and as part of AI solutions for risk. Let us use the same steps to get the input, output, tools, and techniques by applying ML/AI approaches.

Plan

For planning, the ML/AI approach is not considered.

Input:

- Charter
- Management plan

- Risk supporting documents
- Industry policy and standards
- Technology policy and standards
- Risk policy and standards
- Organization rules, regulations, and policy
- Datasets

Tools and techniques:

- Human expertise
- Data analysis
- Meetings and collaboration

Output:

- Risk plan

Identify

- To identify, the ML/AI approach is considered in the risk identification/threat model.

Input:

- Management plan
- Risk supporting documents
- Industry policy and standards
- Technology policy and standards
- Risk policy and standards
- Organization rules, regulations, and policy
- ISO risk standards 31000
- Dataset

Tools and techniques:

- Human expertise
- Data gathering
- Data analysis
- Meetings and collaboration

- Skills and scoring model
- Classification models
- Probabilistic model
- ML and AI models

Output:

- Risk Register
- Risk Report

Qualify

To qualify, the ML/AI approach is considered in the risk categorization/ classification model to predict the risk-impact score and the risk-probability-occurrence score.

Input:

- Management plan
- Risk supporting documents
- Industry policy and standards
- Technology policy and standards
- Risk policy and standards
- Organization rules, regulations, and policy
- ISO Risk standards 31000
- Dataset
- Risk Register

Tools and techniques:

- Human expertise
- Data gathering
- Data analysis
- Meetings and collaboration
- Skills and scoring model
- Classification models
- Probabilistic model
- AI models

Output:
- Risk policy

Quantify

To quantify, the ML/AI approach is considered in the risk categorization/classification model, to predict the risk-impact score, and the risk-probability-occurrence score.

Input:

- Management plan
- Risk supporting documents
- Industry policy and standards
- Technology policy and standards
- Risk policy and standards
- Organization rules, regulations, and policy
- ISO Risk standards 31000
- Dataset
- Risk Register
- Risk Report
- Risk policy

Tools and techniques:

- Human expertise
- Data gathering
- Data analysis
- Meetings and collaboration
- Skills and scoring model
- Classification models
- Probabilistic model
- AI models

Output:
- Risk policy

Respond

To respond, the ML/AI approach is considered in risk mitigation strategy recommendations and risk-contingency recommendations.

Input:

- Management plan
- Risk supporting documents
- Industry policy and standards
- Technology policy and standards
- Risk policy and standards
- Organization rules, regulations, and policy
- ISO risk standards 31000
- Dataset
- Risk Register
- Risk Report
- Risk policy
- Data of risk strategies for threats
- Data of risk strategies for opportunities
- Data of risk strategies for contingent response
- Data of strategies for overall risk

Tools and techniques:

- Human expertise
- Data gathering
- Data analysis
- Meetings and collaboration
- Skills and scoring model
- Strategies for threats
- Strategies for opportunities
- Strategies for contingent response
- Strategies for overall risk
- Classification models
- Probabilistic model

- ML/AI models
- Strategies-recommendation AI model
- Decision-making process

Output:

- Strategies recommendation
- Decision recommendation
- Human takeover

Implement

For implementation, the ML/AI approach is considered in all ML/AI solutions to integrate with the application the business user can use directly.

Input:

- Management plan
- Risk supporting documents
- Industry policy and standards
- Technology policy and standards
- Risk policy and standards
- Organization rules, regulations, and policy
- ISO Risk standards 31000
- Dataset
- Risk Register
- Risk Report
- Risk policy
- Data of risk strategies for threats
- Data of risk strategies for opportunities
- Data of risk strategies for contingent response
- Data of strategies for overall risk
- Respond to process outputs
  o Strategies recommendations
  o Decision recommendations

Tools and techniques:

- Human expertise

- Data gathering
- Data analysis
- Meetings and collaboration
- Skills and scoring model
- Strategies for threats
- Strategies for opportunities
- Strategies for contingent response
- Strategies for overall risk
- Classification models
- Probabilistic model
- ML/AI models
- Strategies recommendation AI model
- Decision-making process

Output:

- Strategies recommendations
- Decision recommendations
- Implementation recommendations
- Human takeover

Monitor and Control

To monitor and control, ML/AI approaches are considered regular data analytics and monitoring through dashboards and scorecards. These scorecards will be used as input to the ML/AI model to mitigate the risk [Note: This is a visionary approach to be automated through the ML/AI approach.].

Input:

- Management plan
- Risk supporting documents
- Industry policy and standards
- Technology policy and standards
- Risk policy and standards
- Organization rules, regulations, and policy
- ISO Risk standards 31000

- Dataset
- Risk Register
- Risk Report
- Risk policy
- Work-performance data
- Work-performance reports

Tools and techniques:

- Human expertise
- Data gathering
- Data analysis
- Meetings and collaboration
- Skills and scoring model
- Strategies for threats
- Strategies for opportunities
- Strategies for contingent response
- Strategies for overall risk
- Classification models
- Probabilistic model
- ML/AI models
- Strategies recommendation AI model
- Decision-making process
- Audits
- Anomaly detections

Output:

- Audits report
- Anomaly detections report
- Notification
- Human takeover

Data Collection

Overall data collection steps taken to achieve this using the existing PMBOK risk process and other risk standard processes.

Risk Register—Data Sample

General information for capturing risks follow:

Risk name: the risk name for each risk must be unique to properly help with analysis.

Open/closed risk status: Open risks are active risks that may occur. Closed risks are those risks that are no longer active, based on risk response or other factors or measures taken. Closed risks may contain important information and should not be deleted from the Risk Register. For this reason, risks should have been deleted.

Risks, issues, lessons learned: Risks are events that may or may not occur and have a probability between 0.0 and 1.0. Issues are events that have already occurred and require a response. Lessons learned are events that occurred in the past and have a history associated with them. It is important to note that inserting new records to the Risk Register may tend to be a risk.

Note that the risk statement, objectives, assumption, cause, and trigger contain textual information about risks, and this can be used in reporting.

Risk mitigation strategy: Such a strategy is required for every identified risk. Mitigation strategies should be entered for positive and negative risks. It is important that the impact and probability are entered.

Risk start and end dates should be entered that show the risk active period.

Risk ID should be added to the Risk Register to provide the uniqueness of the risk.

Note: All columns of the Risk Register should be considered.

Risk Matrix and Risk Trend Chart

Risk matrix and risk trend views are used to determine the severity of a risk and to analyze how risks are changing over time.

The risk matrix is a tool that determines the severity of a risk. The risk matrix view shows severity using risk probability with calculated risk impact of the project risks. The risk matrix view has two sections: a table with a list of risks and their actual calculated values for probability, impact, and score. The table puts each risk into the context of the organization's risk threshold or tolerance.

The risk trend illustrates how project risk changes over time. Risk trend can be presented using a bar chart, stack-area chart, or in a table format.

Risk history illustrates the probability and impact of individual risk and how it has changed over time.

Data Sample

A list of data samples follows:

- Assumption log
- Issue log
- Risk Register
- Duration estimates
- Lessons Learned Register
- Requirements documentation
- Stakeholder Register
- Activity attributes
- Activity lists
- Basis of estimates
- Change log
- Cost estimates
- Cost forecasts
- Milestone list
- Physical resource list
- Project calendars
- Project communications
- Project schedule
- Project schedule network diagram
- Project scope statement
- Project team assignments
- Quality control measurements
- Quality metrics
- Quality report
- Requirement documentation
- Requirement traceability matrix
- Resource breakdown structure

- Risk Register
- Risk Report
- Schedule data
- Schedule forecasts
- Test and evaluation documents
- Team charter
- Work breakdown structure

In forthcoming chapters, we explain each of the previous risk processes in detail to show how AI can be applied.

CHAPTER 6

Identify Risk or Threat Model

Define Goal

Define the goal of the artificial intelligence (AI) model for risk identification or the threat model.

The goal is to identify the risk associated with the application area using standard identification; instead, use AI/machine learning (ML) to automate the process.

See Figure 6.1.

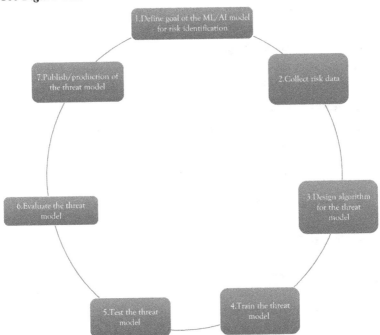

Figure 6.1 Identify the risk or threat model

Figure 6.2 Evaluation steps to identify risk

Now let us evaluate stores and store sales performance to continue, close down, or improve sales.

Evaluation Steps

Let us go through one measure: key performance indicator (KPI) of sales performance in the following example. For simplicity see Figure 6.2. We consider the retail industry in this example to illustrate the steps involved in identifying risk.

Evaluation Measure or KPI

From the given measure or KPI, we consider the retail industry and sales transaction amount as the measure from a point of sale (POS) dataset. One important fueling point for any corporation or store is at the POS transactions in the store. POS indicates when people check out of the store and pay. Analysts can consider many important measures and KPIs to evaluate risk. Planning is required to show how measures/KPI can be used to identify the risk process. Similarly, it can be automated to evaluate other measures and KPIs.

Input:
- List of measures and KPI

Output:
- Identified risk measures list

Evaluate the Business Process

From the given business process, consider the retail industry and POS transaction business process. In the POS business process, KPIs reside in multiple dimensions and measures.

In this step of evaluating the business process, the input and expected output follows.

Input:
- List of business processes and measures/KPIs.

Expected output:
- Identified risk measures listed as business processes.

Steps:
- Feed all measures of the given business process to train the model.

Evaluate Given Dataset

From the given dataset (retail industry|POS dataset) do the following in order:

Identify the business process > identify the list of measures > identify the risk

Evaluate Project-Related Documents

From given project-related documents: Collect the data

Define Risk Identification Steps

Let us take an example of an analytical step of evaluation of stores.
There are three possibilities of actions:

- Store is doing very well and continues to operate and keep up sales.
- Store is not making adequate sales, determines the overall loss, and comes up a strategy going forward.
- Store is just doing ok and is meeting its breakeven point. The store has a possibility of increasing sales. The store performs well in sales, then continues to strategize to keep up the sales.

Let us get into data collection now.

Data Collection

Collect Risk Data

Collect the appropriate dataset associated with the application area. The dataset will have to be collected by resources working in the application area. This includes KPIs and key risk indicators (KRIs).

Input:

- Risk management plan.
- Risk supporting documents.
  - Historically identified risk datasets such as historical data of past risk occurrences, and impact and mitigation actions taken.
- Industry policy and standards.
  - Retail industry standard KPIs such as minimum, maximum, average of industry level KPIs with KRIs from retail industry statistics.
- Technology policy and standards.
  - POS terminal performance data such as system slowness and network slowness.
- Risk policy and standards.
- POS terminal secured network access log data.
- Organization-specific policies and standards.
  - Organization survival minimum requirements data such as revenue going below 40 percent for three months continuously, then closing down the store. Similarly, all other business rules are governed by the organization governance department.
  - Hacker-avoidance policies.
  - Organization rules, regulations, and policies.
- ISO Risk standards 31000.
  - risk categorization documents.
- Dataset
  - POS transaction dataset [use this dataset for training and explanation purposes].

Design Algorithm

Determine appropriate algorithms based on the risk dataset. Conduct further research on how the algorithm can be designed to fit the data.

Identify Features

Identify features from the POS transaction dataset, considering only the important features to explain what is going on.

From the POS transaction dataset:

- Sales transaction amount, store name, store location, transaction date (measures and attributes in the POS transaction dataset).

From unstructured documents:

- Extract data from unstructured documents such as risk plan documents and other word documents using natural language processing to convert to natural language understanding.

From retail industry statistics:

- Retail industry average sales transaction amount by category, store location, and month.

From organization rules document:

- Minimum monthly sales decreased percent considered negative risk.

From the risk standards document:

- Month revenue decrease

From risk supporting documents:

- Past sales transaction amount, risk flag, impact, and action taken

Output:

- Is there a risk or not?
- Determine true or false

ML/AI use case:

ML/AI is a binary classification ML problem using supervised learning. Now we do a deep dive into the binary classification steps.

Identify a List of Binary Classification Models

Here is the typical list of algorithms used for binary classification.
   Deep learning algorithms

- Convolution Neural Network
- Recurrent Neural Network
- Hierarchical Attention Network
   Ensemble
- Random Forest
   Neural Networks
- Radial Basis Function Network
- Perceptron
- Back-Propagation
- Hopfield Network
   Support Vector Machine (SVM)
- Multiclass SVM
   Regression
- Logistic regression
   Bayesian
- Naive Bayes
   Decision Tree
- Classification and Regression Tree
- Conditional Decision Trees
   Dimensionality Reduction
- Quadratic Discriminant Analysis
- Linear Discriminant Analysis (LDA)
   Instance based
- K-Nearest Neighbors

You can pick up more algorithms to be considered to train and evaluate. For simplicity, limiting the following algorithms for binary classification problem.

- LDA
- Quadratic Discriminant Analysis
- Logistic regression

Let's get into data preparation steps from the POS transaction dataset.

Data Preparation

The sample here is the sample dataset considered in our experiment. See Table 6.1.

Table 6.1 Sample Data for Risk Identification Use Case

• Features: all columns except RISK
• Expected output: RISK column
• Input all the features in the above dataset and find feature scoring for the test dataset.
• Identify important features, train with identified features, and find scoring for the test dataset.
• Create bias/variance adjustment for the training dataset to avoid the influence of dominant class (to avoid overfitting/underfitting)
• Split the dataset into three sets as follows:
o Training dataset (60 percent)
o Test dataset (20 percent)
o Validation dataset (20 percent)
• Train/test/validate the model
• Use the identified datasets to train the model.

Train the Model

Train the selected algorithms using the prepared dataset.

Tune the Model

Tune the hyperparameters to train the model

Run the training multiple times with different combinations of provided hyperparameters of batch size, epochs, optimizer, learn rate, momentum, and dropout rate to find the optimum combination of hyperparameters to determine the appropriate results.

- Batch size = [10, 20, 40, 60, 80, 100]
- epochs = [10, 50, 100]
- optimizer = ['SGD', 'RMSprop', 'Adagrad', 'Adadelta', 'Adam', 'Adamax', 'Nadam']
- learn rate = [0.001, 0.01, 0.1, 0.2, 0.3]
- momentum = [0.0, 0.2, 0.4, 0.6, 0.8, 0.9]
- dropout rate = [0.0, 0.1, 0.2, 0.3, 0.4, 0.5, 0.6, 0.7, 0.8, 0.9]

By using Grid Search() you can automate to try out different combinations of hyperparameters. It is recommended to use Grid Search().

grid search = GridSearchCV(estimator=model, param_grid=param_grid, n_jobs=-1, scoring=accuracy)

Compare models with different hyperparameters, choose the best fit hyperparameters, and use the model to train further with the full dataset.

Test the Model

Test the model using the test dataset for each selected algorithm with given methods:

- Specify the used loss function with respective algorithms.
- Learning rate curve.
- Learning curve.

Loss versus epoch—learning rate graph. See Figure 6.3. Pick the model with the "learning rate- Good" depicted in the graph.

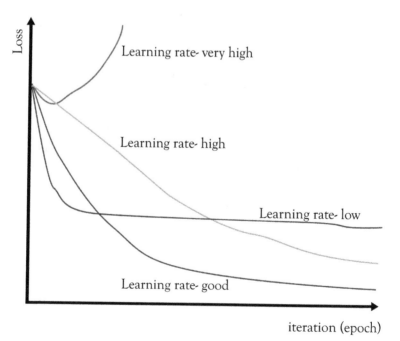

Figure 6.3 Loss versus epoch learning graph

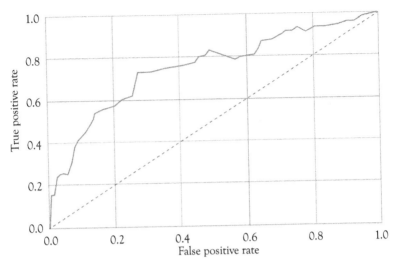

Figure 6.4 *ROC curve*

Receiver Operating Characteristic Curve

Receiver operating characteristic (ROC) is another common tool used with binary classifiers. See Figure 6.4. For this use case, we choose the model with a false positive rate as 0.99 because we expect 90 percent accuracy from identify risk or threat model.

Evaluate the Model

Evaluate the model using accuracy, mean square error, and determine the learning rate. The following scoring methods are used.

Scoring Methods

- Precision score
- Recall score
- F1 score
- Support score
- Accuracy score
- Area under the curve/ROC
- Learning rate (ranges from 0 to 1)

Confusion Matrix

- Analyze the inputs that are improperly classified using the confusion matrix.
- Accuracy versus epoch graph.
- Decide the final model with accuracy.

Repeat steps from data collection to data preparation, feature extraction, training, testing, and evaluation of the model until reaching the necessary accuracy of 85 and above.

Model Conclusion

Based on accuracy and F1 score, linear discriminant analysis is the best performing model for this binary classification problem of risk identification. See Table 6.2.

Binary Classification Methods Comparison

Publish/Production of the Model

- Retrain the model until it yields the desired output.
  - ○ Repeat the steps from data collection, data preparation, feature extraction, training, testing, and evaluation of the model; then publish the model.
  - ○ Repeat the entire process for all measures in this business process, as explained in the evaluation steps.

Table 6.2 Model score comparison

Model	Accuracy	Precision	Recall	F1 score	AUC ROC
Linear discriminant analysis	0.948757	0.959455	0.928571	0.947142	0.993056
Quadratic discriminant analysis	0.94348	0.939012	0.941415	0.943893	0.989324
Logistic regression	0.943348	0.945292	0.932303	0.943039	0.989973
Random Forest	0.941126	0.944909	0.928457	0.940401	0.982154
K-Nearest Neighbors	0.935848	0.943361	0.916987	0.93403	0.954365
Bayes	0.930994	0.931379	0.917903	0.930448	0.97938

Note. AUC = area under the curve, ROC = receiver operating characteristic.

- Possible ways to productionalize the trained model follow.
  ○ Host in Google cloud, Microsoft Azure, or AWS.
- How do we deploy the trained model?
  https://cloud.google.com/ml-engine/docs/tensorflow/deploying-models
- Regularly monitor and update the model.
- How do we use the productionalized model for business users?
  ○ Integrate the trained model with the application for business users to identify new risks or threats from the new dataset.

Conclusion

Types of resources needed for this project follow:

- Risk analysis subject matter expert.
- Risk mitigation strategists
- Data analysts
- Data architects
- Data scientists
- Data engineers
  Simplify all of the previous steps in www.BizStats.AI
  To automate, following are the steps to be done
- Provide the input dataset
- Train multiple models
- Present models with accuracy
- Pick the model and activate it
- The business user can directly use it just by searching.

CHAPTER 7

Risk Categorization/ Classification Model

Define the Goal

Define the goal of the model for the risk categorization/classification model.

The goal is to categorize and classify risks associated with the application area using artificial intelligence (AI)/machine learning (ML) to automate the process. The output from a previous risk identification model is the input to this risk categorization.

Evaluation Steps

Follow the risk identification model evaluation steps in a similar manner. See Figure 7.1.

Evaluate Measure or Key Performance Indicator

Input:
- List measures and key performance indicator (KPI) and risk measures identified in Step 1 of identified risk

Output:
- List identified risk measures with their risk category names

Figure 7.1 Evaluation steps for risk categorization

Evaluate Business Processes

Input:
- List business processes and measures/KPIs with identified risks.

Output:
- List identified risk measures in business processes in the risk category.

Identify the list of measures > Identify the risks list > identify the list of categories.

Steps:
- Feed all identified measures of the given business process from "identify risk model" to train the model.

Evaluate the Given Dataset

From the given dataset (retail industry|POS dataset)

Identify the business process > identify the list of measures > identify the risk

Input:
- Feed all identify-list-of-risk measures identified in the "identify risk or threat model" step.

Output:
- List respective risk category names

Identify the business process > Identify the list of measures > Identify the risks list > Identify the list of categories.

Evaluate Project-Related Documents

Collect the data from the given project-related documents.

Now we go into data collection to collect risk category data.

Data Collection

Collect Risk Category Data

Collecting a risk category dataset associated with the application area may require labeling category data based on identified risks manually process to maintain as the input.

Input:
- Output of the risk identification model.

Design Algorithm

Design an algorithm for the risk categorization model.

The risk categorization model is a typical classification of an ML problem. Thus, apply the classification algorithm.

Output is to which risk category the identified risk measure belongs. That is the risk category name.

ML/AI use case:

This is called the multiclass classification ML problem using supervised learning. Now we dive deeply into multiclass classification steps.

Identify the List of Multiclass Classification Models

Here is the list of typical algorithms used for a multiclass classification ML problem.

- K-nearest neighbors
- Naive Bayes
- Decision trees
- Support Vector Machine (SVM)
- Random Forest
- Decomposing into binary classification
  - One-versus-all
  - All-versus-all
- Hierarchical clustering
- Hierarchical SVM

- Neural networks
- Deep learning (with softmax technique)
  - Convolution Neural Network (CNN)
  - Recurrent Neural Network (RNN)
  - Hierarchical attention network

Finalized Algorithm for a Multiclass Classification Problem

For our experiment, we limit ourselves to only the following algorithms:

- RNN
- CNN
- GaussianNB Classifier

Data Preparation

As discussed in the ML/AI project chapter in the data preparation section, we discussed a need for preparation to avoid oversampling and undersampling.

- Oversampling/undersampling techniques are used to adjust the class distribution in the dataset.
- Apply the dimensionality reduction technique as part of the data preparation step.

The goal is to reduce the number of features to be examined in the model evaluation process. For example, if risk categories are more than 10, apply the dimensionality reduction process to reduce it to below 10.

Apply any one of the following dimensionality reduction techniques to limit number of possibilities to experiment. This goes to time versus cost versus usefulness.

List of dimensionality reduction techniques:

- Principal component analysis (PCA)
- Non-negative matrix factorization
- Kernel PCA

- Graph-based kernel PCA
- Linear Discriminant Analysis
- Generalized discriminant analysis
- Autoencoder

Measure risk name	Change percentage	Risk category
Sales amount decrease	−10%	Financial/competitive risk
Sales amount increase	30%	Inventory risk

Train the Model

Use the identified datasets to train the model.

- Split the dataset into three sets as follows:
  - Training dataset (60 percent)
  - Test dataset (20 percent)
  - Validation dataset (20 percent)
- Tuning the hyperparameters to train the model as before to identify the risk model.
- Use the trained model for multiple iterations with 100 epochs per iteration.
- Use the trained model for various combinations of features to find the best model.

Tune the Model

Tune the hyperparameters to train the model.

Run the training multiple times with different combinations of the hyperparameters of selected algorithms. Typically use batch size, epochs, optimizer, learn rate, momentum, and dropout rate to find the optimum combination of hyperparameters to determine the appropriate results.

Compare models with different hyperparameters and choose the best fit hyperparameters; use the model to train further with the full dataset.

Test the Model

Same as identify risk or threat model testing, expect this to be a multiclass classification model.

Evaluate the Model

Evaluate the model using accuracy and mean square error, and determine the learning rate.

Performance analysis steps.

Use a Confusion Matrix

A confusion matrix measures the performance of classification algorithms. Refer to Figure 7.2.

- X—Predicted Value [Risk Categories]—5 (1 to 5)
- Y—Targeted Value [Target Categories]—5 (1 to 5)

Use encoded values instead of actual risk categories.

	Category A	Category B	Category C	Category D	Category E	
Category A	70	5	7	9	9	100
Category B	2	77	6	8	7	
Category C	4	4	80	5	7	50
Category D	7	3	2	79	9	
Category E	2	5	3	18	72	0

Figure 7.2 Confusion matrix predicted versus targeted

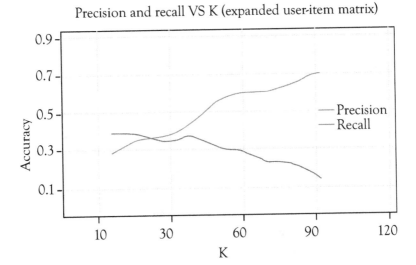

Figure 7.3 Precision and recall versus K

Precision–Recall Curves

Precision–recall curves measure the success of the classification model (refer to Figure 7.3).

Check mistakes of the classification model on each label and analyze to fine-tune (refer to Figure 7.4).

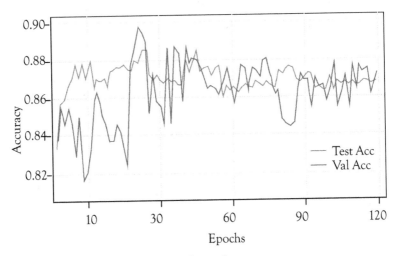

Figure 7.4 Accuracy versus epoch graph

Accuracy Versus Epoch Graph

Decide the final model with accuracy

- If the classification prediction is wrong, you can improve the accuracy by using more training data. Collect more data, then retrain the classification and reevaluate the model for improvement in accuracy.
- If the "classification prediction is wrong because of wrong training data," use the urAI-text annotation tool (https://biz-stats.ai/product/urAI.html) to correct the input training data, then retrain the classification and reevaluate the model for improvement in accuracy.
- Another method to evaluate model accuracy uses ensemble learning methods.
- Ensemble learning methods are
- Sequential ensemble methods
- Parallel ensemble methods
- A combination of both
- Weighted majority rule ensemble classifier

The final ensemble classifier method is the "weighted majority rule ensemble classifier," based on our experiments. This provides better accuracy than any other ensemble method. Here, we look deeply into this method and how it is done.

Weighted Majority Rule Ensemble Classifier

We use three different classification models to classify the samples logistic regression, a naive Bayes classifier with a Gaussian kernel, and a random forest classifier, combined into an ensemble method.

- Cross-validation (five-fold cross-validation) results provide the following:
  - Accuracy: 0.90 (±0.05) [logistic regression]
  - Accuracy: 0.92 (±0.05) [random forest]
  - Accuracy: 0.91 (±0.04) [naive Bayes]

These cross-validation results show that the performance of the three models is almost equal.

Now, we implement a simple ensemble classifier class that allows us to combine the three different classifiers. Define a predict method that simply takes the majority rule of the predictions by the classifiers. For example, if the prediction for a sample is

- Classifier 1 → class 1
- Classifier 2 → class 1
- Classifier 3 → class 2

Now, classify the sample as "class 1."

Furthermore, add a weights parameter. We assign a specific weight to each classifier. To work with the weights, collect the predicted class probabilities for each classifier, multiply it by the classifier weight, and take the average. Based on these weighted average probabilities, we assign the class label.

To illustrate this with a simple example, we assume three classifiers and three-class classification problems to assign equal weights to all classifiers (the default): $w1 = 1$, $w2 = 1$, and $w3 = 1$.

We then calculate the weighted average probabilities for a sample as follows (see Table 7.1).

As in Table 7.1, class 2 has the highest weighted average probability; thus, we classify the sample as class 2.

- Accuracy: 0.90 (±0.05) [logistic regression]
- Accuracy: 0.92 (±0.05) [random forest]
- Accuracy: 0.91 (±0.04) [naive Bayes]
- Accuracy: 0.95 (±0.03) [ensemble]

Table 7.1 Weighted average calculation

Classifier Name	Class 1	Class 2	Class 3
Classifier 1	W1 * 0.2	W1* 0.5	W1 * 0.3
Classifier 2	W1 * 0.6	W1* 0.3	W1 * 0.1
Classifier 3	W1 * 0.3	W1* 0.4	W1 * 0.3
Weighted average	0.37	0.4	0.3

Table 7.2 Prediction based on majority class label

Classifier Name	Class 1	Class 2
Classifier 1	1	0
Classifier 1	0	1
Classifier 1	0	1
Prediction	-	1

We use the ensemble classifier class to apply to majority voting, purely on the class labels, if no weights are provided and are the predicted probability values otherwise. Prediction builds on majority class labels.

Prediction based on majority class labels (Table 7.2):

Prediction based on predicted probabilities:

This is for equal weights, weights = [1,1,1]. See Table 7.3.

The results differ depending on whether one applies a majority vote based on the class labels or takes the average of predicted probabilities. In general, it makes more sense to use the predicted probabilities (scenario 2). Here, a "very confident" classifier 1 overrules the very unconfident classifiers 2 and 3.

Returning to our weight's parameter, we use a naive brute-force approach to find the optimal weights for each classifier to increase prediction accuracy (Table 7.4).

Final words: When applying the ensemble classifier to the previous example, the results surely looked nice. But must keep in mind that this is just a toy example. The majority rule voting approach might not always work as well in practice, especially if the ensemble consists of more "weak" than "strong" classification models. Here, use a cross-validation approach

Table 7.3 Weighted average with prediction

Classifier	Class 1	Class 2
Classifier 1	0.99	0.01
Classifier 2	0.49	0.51
Classifier 3	0.49	0.51
Weighted average	0.66	0.18
Prediction	1	-

Table 7.4 Example of a comparison table

Iteration	W1	W2	W3	Mean	Standard deviation
2	1	2	2	0.953333	0.033993
17	3	1	2	0.953333	0.033993
20	3	2	2	0.946667	0.045216

to overcome the overfitting challenge. Please always keep a spare validation dataset to evaluate the results.

Model Conclusion

Based on our experiment, the "Weighted Majority Rule Ensemble Classifier" Ensemble performs better than other algorithms for the risk categorization/classification model.

Publish/Production of the Model

Publish/produce the model, as in identify risk or threat model.

Conclusion

Same as the conclusion of the identify risk or threat model.

CHAPTER 8

Predicting Risk Impact Score Model

Define Goal

Define the goal of the model for predicting the risk impact score model. Predict the impact of risk based on expert knowledge or derived from historical occurrences.

Evaluation Steps

Evaluation Measure or Key Performance Indicator

From a given measure

Input:
- Risk measure identified in the "risk categorization/classification" step.

Output:
- Risk impact score 1 to 10 (minimum to high)

Evaluate the Business Process

From the given business process (retail industry Ex: sales transaction)

Input:
- Feed the list of risk measures identified in the "risk categorization/classification" step.

Output:

- List respective risk impact scores

Identify the list of measures > Identify the risks list > Identify the list of risk impact scores

Evaluate Given Dataset

From given data (retail industry Ex: POS data)

Input:

- Feed the list of risk measures identified in the "risk categorization/classification" step.

Output:

- List the respective risk impact scores

Identify the business process > Identify the list of measures > Identify the risks list > Identify the list of risk impact scores.

Evaluate Project-Related Documents

From the given project-related documents:

Collect risk impact data from historical occurrences or from an expert.

Use expert knowledge to capture the system of annotation and historical dataset.

Input:
- Management plan
  - Evaluate stores and store sales performance to continue, close down, or improve sales.
- Risk supporting documents
  - Historically identified risk datasets (past risk faced, its impact, and mitigation action taken).

- Risk policy and standards
  - Company survival minimum requirements data (if revenue goes below 40 percent for three months, close down the company).
  - Hacker-avoidance policies
- Organization rules, regulations, and policy
  - Organization rules (ex: monthly sales below 20 percent is a negative risk).
- Dataset
  - POS transaction dataset

Data Collection

Input:
- Output of risk categorization/classification model.
  - Measure risk name
  - Sales
  - Store
  - Location
  - Date
  - Industry average sales prev month
  - Industry average sales prev month – 1
  - Minimum monthly sales decrease percent
  - Three-month revenue decrease
  - Past sales transaction amount
  - Past risk flag
  - Past impact score
  - Past action taken
  - Risk category

Output:
- What is the risk impact score?
- Risk impact score (1 to 10)

Design Algorithm

Design an Algorithm to Predict the Risk Impact

The impact score is based on a range of numbers, typically 1 to 10; 1 means minimal impact and 10 means maximum impact. The corporation determines the range and impact based on expert knowledge related to the risk. The goal of predicting an algorithm is to determine whole numbers ranging from 1 to 10, based on historical data and expert knowledge through human annotation.

ML/AI Use Case

The machine learning (ML)/artificial intelligence (AI) use case is a regression analysis with continuous dependent variables. Now, we dive deeply into the regression steps.

Identify the List of Regression Models

The following algorithms can be used for regression analysis with continuous dependent variables (Table 8.1 and 8.2)

- Linear regression
- Polynomial regression
- Stepwise regression and best subsets regression
- Least absolute shrinkage and selection operator (LASSO) regression
- Ridge regression
- Partial least squares
  - Nonlinear regression
  - Support Vector Machine (SVM) with a nonlinear kernel
  - Quantile regression
  - Bayesian inference
  - Gauss–Newton algorithm
  - Gradient descent algorithm
  - Levenberg–Marquardt algorithm

Finalized
- Polynomial regression
- SVM with a nonlinear kernel
- Deep neural networks (deep learning)

Data Preparation

Table 8.1 Sample data prep

Measure risk name	Risk Category	Change Percentage	Risk Impact Score
Sales amount decrease	Financial/competitive risk	−10%	10
Sales amount increase	Inventory risk	30%	5

Table 8.2 Data sample with all features

Risk name (from step 1)	Sales Amount Decrease
Sales amount	10M
Store name	store1
Location	Atlanta
Date	1/3/18
Industry average sales amount previous month	30M
Industry average sales amount previous month − 1	40M
Minimum monthly sales amount decrease percent	15%
Three-month revenue decrease	20%
Past sales transaction amount	5M
Past risk flag	Y
Risk impact	High
Action taken	Store closed
Risk impact score (label)	10

Data Preprocessing

- Missing values in categorical variables (e.g., store or location) need to be corrected or removed.

- Reduce some levels if categorical predictors have many levels. A store has thousands of stores, so, group them based on sales volume and reduce them to three to five levels.
- When using hundreds of variables, no regression will be interpretable. Reduce the number of variables using LASSO or least angle regression, factor analysis, substantive knowledge, correlation matrices, principal component analysis, or partial least squares.

Start with sensitivity analysis. Check the influence of each independent variable on the dependent(s) variable. Try to find out how much you can change each independent variable to change the dependent(s) by (for example) 10 percent.

For continuous variables: Use Pearson correlation coefficients. If Pearson correlation is near 1 or –1 among two, one should disappear in multiple regression (Figure 8.1).

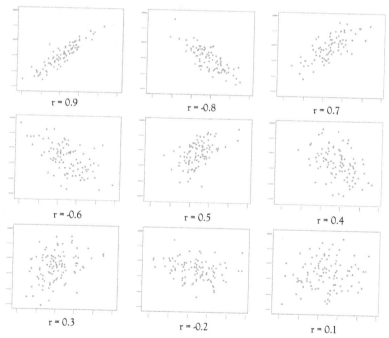

Figure 8.1 Pearson correlation scatter plot

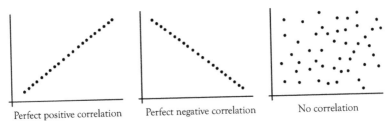

Perfect positive correlation   Perfect negative correlation   No correlation

Figure 8.2 Correlation sample

For category variables: If most counts appear in the diagonal of the contingency table, one of the two category variables should disappear. Draw scatter plots with continuous outcomes to see the association. Confirm if a linear trend is shown, the factor is in, if a nonlinear effect is shown, or transformation is needed. If no trend emerges, like the scatter plot is random, the independent factor could be out of sync (Figure 8.2).

Using 14 variables, reduce it to 7 variables using aforementioned dimensionality reduction technique. The reduced variables list follows:

- Measure risk name
- Sales
- Store
- Risk category
- Industry average sales previous month
- Industry average sales previous month – 1
- Minimum monthly sales decrease percent

Check for outliers by leverage or CooksD or Residual. If outliers are present, we can delete them to improve the quality of the data (Figure 8.3).

Check normality. If violated, use transformation on some independent factor. If variance homogeneity exists, transform the dependent factor. These processes may improve model fitting.

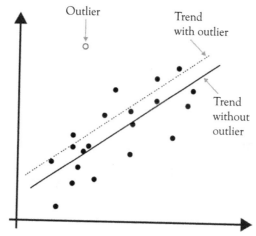

Figure 8.3 Trend with or without outlier

Train the Model

Using Deep Neural Network Architecture

Here we train the deep neural network to predict the risk impact score. We present details of deep neural network architecture for this risk impact score model.

See Figure 2.6 for the deep neural network.

Activation function: see Figure 8.4.

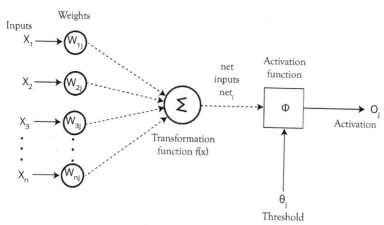

Figure 8.4 Activation function of neural network

Table 8.3 Deep neural network layers

Layer (type)	Output Shape	Param #
Input layer (Dense)	(none, 128)	19,200
Hidden layer 1 (Dense)	(none, 256)	33,024
Hidden layer 1 (Dense)	(none, 256)	65,792
Hidden layer 1 (Dense)	(none, 256)	65,792
Output layer (Dense)	(none, 1)	257

Note: Total params:184,065; trainable params:184,065; nontrainable params: 0.

This deep neural network consists of

- One input layer with 14 nodes.
- Three hidden layers with 256 nodes each with a "relu" activation function and a "normal" initializer as the kernal_intializer.
- Mean absolute error is a loss function.
- The output layer has only one node.
- Use "linear" as the activation function for the output layer (refer to Figure 8.4 and Table 8.3).

See that the validation loss of the best model is 18520.23 (Figure 8.5).

```
[out]:
Train on 1168 samples, validate on 292 samples
Epoch 1/500
1168/1168 [==========================] - 0s 266us/step -loss:
19251.8903 - mean_absolute_error: 19251.8903 - val_loss: 23041.8968
- val_mean_absolute_error: 23041.8968
Epoch 0001: val_loss did not improve from 21730.9355
Epoch 2/500
1168/1168 [==========================] - 0s 268us/step -loss:
19251.8903 - mean_absolute_error: 18300.8433 - val_loss: 22324.8762
- val_mean_absolute_error: 21231.8968
Epoch 0002: val_loss did not improve from 21730.9355



.
.
.
Epoch 0500: val_loss did not improve from 18520.2376
```

Figure 8.5 Training log output

Using Other Algorithms

Use the identified datasets to train the model with an annotated dataset.

Fit a model using linear regression first, then determine whether the linear model provides an adequate fit by *checking the residual plots*. If you cannot obtain a good fit using linear regression, try a nonlinear model because it can fit a wider variety of curves. We recommend using ordinary least squares first because it is easier to perform and interpret.

Use Akaike's information criterion, Bayesian information criterion, or Mallows' CP to decide how many factors should be included (Figure 8.6). Using them is better than comparing R^2.

Perform multiple regression. If the sample size is large enough, you may use the autoselect option, such as forward, backward, or best, which will select independent factors using sampling techniques.

Use sampling techniques.

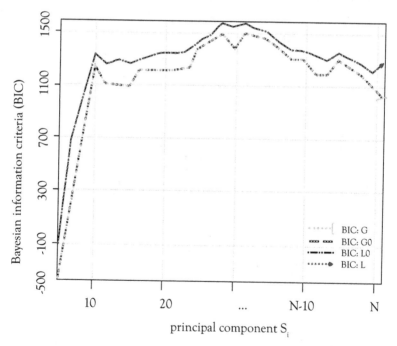

Figure 8.6 Principal components versus Bayesian information criterion

Test the Model

Test the model using the test dataset and expert knowledge.

Analyze different metrics like the statistical significance of parameters, R^2, adjusted R^2, Akaike information criterion, Bayesian information criterion, and the error term (Figure 8.7). Another one to use is *Mallow's Cp* criterion, which checks for possible bias in the model by comparing the model with all possible submodels (or a careful selection of them).

The model on the left is more accurate.

If the dataset has multiple confounding variables, you should not choose an automatic model selection method because you do not want to put these in a model at the same time.

Regression regularization methods (LASSO, Ridge, and ElasticNet) work well in case of high dimensionality and multicollinearity among the variables in the dataset.

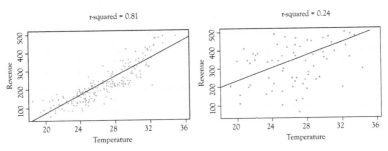

Figure 8.7 *R^2 comparison graph*

Evaluate the Model

Evaluate the model using accuracy and mean square error and determine the learning rate. Cross-validation is the best way to evaluate models used for prediction. Here, divide the dataset into two groups (train and validate). A simple mean squared difference between the observed and predicted values gives a measure to predict accuracy (Figure 8.8).

Good vs bad ML cross validation

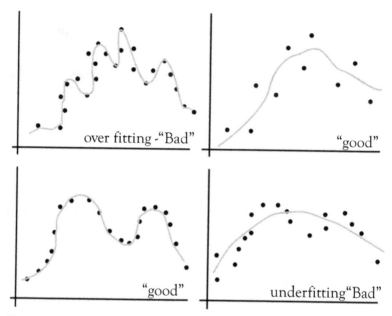

Figure 8.8 Cross-validation comparison

Cross-validation graph:

Predicting the risk impact score model using a linear model:

Check predicted versus actual and root mean square error (RMSE) score as follows (Figure 8.9).

Test RMSE score: 5.125877

Predicting the risk impact score model using bagged model using a randomForest algorithm:

Now, fit a bagged model using the randomForest algorithm. Bagging is a special case of a random forest where mtry (the number of variables randomly sampled as candidates at each split) is equal to p, the number of predictors. Try using 13 predictors.

Test RMSE score: 3.843966.

See two interesting results. First, the predicted versus actual plot no longer has a small number of predicted values. Second, the test error has dropped dramatically. Also note that the "mean of squared residuals," which is output from randomForest, is the out-of-bag (OOB) estimate of the error.

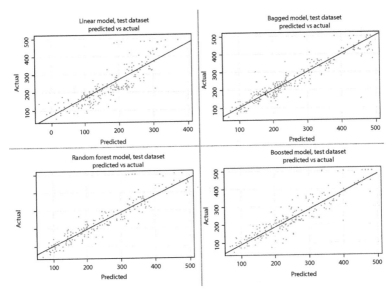

Figure 8.9 Evaluate the ensemble model predicted versus actual

Predicting the risk impact score model using a randomForest algorithm:

Now try using a random forest algorithm. For regression, we suggest using mtry equal to $p/3 = 4$ predictors

Test RMSE score: 3.701805.

Here note three RMSEs. The training RMSE (which is optimistic), the OOB RMSE (which is a reasonable estimate of the test error), and the test RMSE. Also note that we calculated variable importance. See Table 8.4 that is comparison of data and error.

Table 8.4 Data versus error comparison

No	Data	Error
1	Training Data	1.558111
2	OOB	3.576229
3	Test	3.701805

Note. OOB = out-of-bag.

Predicting the risk impact score model using a boosted model:

Last, try using a boosted model, which by default will produce a nice variable importance plot as well as plots of the marginal effects of the predictors. Based on this analysis, decide which variable has a greater influence on the risk impact score.

See Table 8.5 for the results of test error by models.

Table 8.5 Results

	Model	Test Error
1	Single Tree	5.45808
2	Linear Model	5.12587
3	Bagging	3.84396
4	Random Forest	3.70180
5	Boosting	3.43382

Model Conclusion

The ensemble boosting model performed better than other algorithms in predicting a risk impact score.

Publish/Produce the Model

Same as risk categorization.

Conclusion

Same as risk categorization.

The same ML/AI model can be used to score the skills mentioned as follows.

Skills AI Scoring Models

- Being respectfulness score (helping others retain their autonomy)
- Courteousness score
- Friendliness score
- Kindness score
- Honesty score
- Trustworthiness score
- Loyalty score
- Ethical score

Skills scoring models can be used in customer, customer support executives, project resources, vendors, suppliers, buyers, and much more.

CHAPTER 9

Risk Probability Occurrence Model

Determining the probability of occurrences based on expert knowledge and derived from historical occurrences.

Define Goal

Define the goal of the model for risk probability impact.

Evaluation Steps

Evaluate Measure or Key Performance Indicator

From the given measure:

Input:
- Output of the step identified risk or threat.
- Output of the step identified risk category.
- Output of the step predicted risk impact score.

Output:
- Risk occurrence probability (0.0 to 1.0).

Evaluate the Business Process

From the given business process:

Input:
- Feed the list of risk measures identified in the step identified risk or threat.

Output:

- List of respective risk probability.

Identify the list of measures > Identify the risks list > Identify the list of risk occurrence probabilities

Evaluate the Given Dataset

From the given data [retail industry such as point of sale (POS) data].

Input:

- Feed the list of risk measures identified in the step identified risk or threat.

Output:

- List of respective risk probability

Identify the business process > Identify the list of measures > Identify the risks list > Identify the list of risk occurrence probabilities

Evaluate Project-Related Documents

From the given project-related documents:

Collect risk probability data from historical occurrences and from an expert.

By using expert knowledge, capture the system of the annotation tool and historical dataset.

Input:

- Management plan
- Risk supporting documents
- Risk policy and standards
- Organization rules, regulations, and policy

Design Algorithm

Design an algorithm to predict risk probability occurrence.

Identify Features

Identify features from the previous inputs

From the POS transaction dataset:
- Sales transaction amounts, store name, store location, transaction dates (measures and attributes in the POS transaction dataset).

  From unstructured documents:
- Extract using NLP

  From retail industry statistics:
- Retail industry average sales transaction amount by category, store location, and month.

  From the organization rules document:
- Minimum monthly sales decrease percent to be risked.

  From the risk standards document:
- Three-month revenue decrease

  From the risk supporting document:
- Past sales transaction amounts, risk flags, impact, and action taken.

  From previous steps:
- Output from the step identified risk or threat.
- Output from the step identified risk category.
- Output from the step predicted risk-impact score.

Output:
- What is the probability of risk occurrence?
- Risk occurrence probability. The probability of occurrence is based on a range of numbers, typically 0.0 to 1.0 with 0 indicating no occurrence and 1.0 indicating 100 percent predicted events. This is predicting the probabilistic model.

Machine learning (ML)/artificial intelligence (AI) use case:

The ML/AI use case is a regression problem using supervised training. Now we dive deeply into the regression steps.

Identify the List of Regression Models

Same as the step predicting the risk-impact score model

Data Preparation

See Table 9.1 for Sample data risk occurrence probability.

Table 9.1 Sample data risk occurrence probability

Measure Risk Name	Risk Category	Change Percentage	Risk-Impact Score	Risk Occurrence Probability
Sales amount decrease	Financial/ competitive risk	–10%	10	0.20
Sales amount increase	Inventory risk	30%	5	0.46

See Table 9.2 for data all the features.

Table 9.2 Sample data with all features

Risk name (from step 1)	Sales amount decrease
Risk category	Financial/competitive risk
Risk-impact score	10
Sales	10M
Store	store1
Location	Atlanta
Date	43103
Industry average sales prev month	30M
industry average sales prev month – 1	40M
Minimum monthly sales decrease percent	0.15
Three months revenue decrease	0.2
Past sales transaction amount	5M
Past risk flag	Y
Impact	High
Action taken	Store Closed
Risk occurrence probability	0.2

Data Preprocessing

- When a category variable contains many categories, grouping them into smaller numbers of categories would help achieve better training and accuracy.
- Balance imbalanced classes because most ML algorithms work best when the number of samples in each class is about equal.
- When there are many features, keep only the features that are good predictors of the output.
- Remove outliers, if possible, because some algorithms are very sensitive to outliers.
- Use oversampling techniques like synthetic minority oversampling technique algorithms to increase the training samples. Predict variables (desired target):
- Has the risk occurred?
- Value 1 or 0 (1 means "Yes," 0 means "No").
- Derive this from the risk occurrence probability. If the probability is above 0.80, it means 1 else 0.
- This process is based on the company's policy and the application of human intelligence.

Train the Model

Use the identified datasets to train the model with the annotated dataset.

Test the Model

Predict the test set results and calculate accuracy.
Test the accuracy of the logistic regression classifier on the test set: 0.83.
Test the model using the test dataset and expert knowledge.

Evaluate the Model

Evaluate the model using accuracy and mean square error and determine the learning rate.

Confusion Matrix

	Precision	Recall	F1-score	Support
0	0.71	0.80	0.75	7666
1	0.77	0.67	0.72	7675
Avg/total	0.74	0.74	0.74	15341

With the entire test set, 83 percent of the time risk occurred.

Model Conclusion

The logistic regression classifier performed better than other algorithms for the risk probability occurrence model.

Publish/Produce the Model

Same as the predicting risk-impact score model.

Conclusion

Same as the predicting risk-impact score model.

CHAPTER 10

Risk Priority Model

Define the Goal

Define the goal of the model for the risk priority model.

Determine the risk priority based on calculation by multiplying impact by the probability occurrence. The priority will be based on all identified risks and their rankings. The highest ranking will have a priority of 1, and lesser rankings follow in decreasing order.

Data Collection

Data calculation for risk priority.

This value derives from calculations with no need to collect an additional dataset.

Design Algorithm

Design algorithm for risk priority.

Ranking builds on descending order of the calculated value. *No need to train the model.*

Train the Model

No need to train. If additional changes are needed to the risks and ranking, then recalculate and rank. Go back to the identify risk or threat model, the risk categorization/classification model, the predicting risk-impact score model, and the risk-probability occurrence model.

Test the Model

Test the model. If additional changes are needed to the risks and ranking, then recalculate and rank. Go back to the identify risk or threat model, risk categorization/classification model, predicting risk-impact score model, and the risk-probability occurrence model.

Evaluate the Model

No need to evaluate.

Publish/Produce the Model

No need to publish the model.

Conclusion

Risk priority is complete, based on calculations.

CHAPTER 11

Conclusion

The use of artificial intelligence (AI) is becoming prolific these days. One can hear about AI on television, radio, and the Worldwide Internet. The risk has been a topic in everyone's mind and continues to hurt organizations and individuals in the international corporate world, as well as domestically. Here, we recapitulate important reminders that will benefit those in all walks of life.

Risk is not fun to experience. Organizations that have endured risk do not take them lightly. We can go on and on discussing the negative impacts risk has created. We graphically described vivid areas impacted by risk in this book. Do not turn your face away from risks or the negative impacts that come with them. We discussed natural risk at length; natural risk cannot be stopped but can be mitigated to save lives. It is worth paying careful attention to the steps that humans have available to mitigate natural risks.

It is important that risks are identified early and in a timely manner to minimize the impact of damage or fatal situations. Based on discussions laid out in this book, the reader can take advantage of using the tools presented. Risks usually require risk management to safely cope with the situation. The data collected must be used carefully. This may mean going through checklists to ensure appropriate questions are answered and appropriate immediate steps taken, based on the immediate answers. Action may include capturing historical data on risk issues. Once accurate data accrue, the next step is to analyze them carefully and accurately. Captured data may help predict the future occurrence of risk issues. This approach may help salvage nasty situations that can be damaging and expensive to individuals or organizations.

Because risk issues are important, it is important for organizations to understand the hybrid types. Careful analysis will provide accurate direction. We chose AI to provide directions. However, AI requires accurate inputs to gain accurate outputs. The source of data and quality of data are crucial in every way. This book provides various use cases that may be helpful to organizations in properly strategizing the route to take. Organizations must define, analyze, monitor, control, and mitigate risks.

Because humans cannot analyze a huge amount of data or take a long time to process data, data science, data analytics, and machine learning (ML) algorithms are used to analyze data that ultimately will be used as input to determine corrective actions. AI is a legitimate way to carry out all the necessary determinations. Using machines to learn from previous human experiences as data input and enables continuous learning from new sets of input data, based on the development of mathematical algorithms leading to the creation of ML. Subsequently, we used AI in this book. We carried out complete AI system development to clearly illustrate how to process risk data. We provide recommendations for the most effective methods. The methods of data collection and development in this book offer the reader ways to understand how to tackle use cases such as AI and risk in an organization. AI produces effective and dramatic results in business, and organizations desiring to understand and improve risk management skills can use AI to improve their chances of handling risk.

Much evidence has shown that risk management has become important everywhere. Case studies in this book illustrated and supported the use of large volumes of data, different velocities, and varieties of data from various sources. We assess that risk concerns will not stop soon. Rather, they appear to be growing larger and more frequent with sometimes massive negative impact. An undetermined positive risk can also hurt organizations when it comes to business opportunities leading to a loss of revenue. In general, the range and breadth of risk creates havoc across the world and on a variety of projects. We show the importance of risk management in organizations in many sections of this book. The harm of risk, without appropriate management, can be devastating. Using the correct tools can address or prevent that devastation.

We focused much effort on problem statements with appropriate use cases and proposals for use of AI solutions using data science and ML approaches. The comprehensive description of AI and risk provides concrete answers to crucial questions that so many organizations face:

Where are these risks and what can be done to lower their impacts? Is AI part of the answer to risk mitigation? Organizations and individuals may gain much knowledge and shared experiences from this book.

For organizations willing to create their own AI systems for risk, this book will guide them step by step. Additionally, the reader can look at Bizstats.ai for more guidance. Bizstats.ai offers numerous customized AI design tools; individuals and organizations are welcome to contact them. Should the reader need training on the tools used in the implementation of AI and risk, please contact Bizstats.ai.

References

5 Steps to Assess And Mitigate Cyber Security Risks. (n.d.). Retrieved from https://sungardas.com/en/about/resources/articles/5-steps-to-assess-and-mitigate-cyber-security-risks/

AI researcher Ben Goertzel Explains Why He Became Interested in AGI Instead of Narrow AI. Published October 18, 2013. Retrieved 16 February 2014. http://intelligence.org/2013/10/18/ben-goertzel/

Alexander, S. May 22, 2015. *AI Researchers On AI Risk*. Retrieved from https://slatestarcodex.com/2015/05/22/ai-researchers-on-ai-risk/

Alexander, S. May 29, 2015. *No Time Like the Present for AI Safety Work*. Retrieved from https://slatestarcodex.com/2015/05/29/no-time-like-the-present-for-ai-safety-work/

Anna. March-June 28, 2016. *130 Project Risks (List)*. Retrieved from https://management.simplicable.com/management/new/130-project-risks

Argyro Panaretou, M.S. February 10, 2009. *Corporate Risk Management and Hedge Accounting*. (Lancaster University Management School Department of Accounting and Finance) Retrieved from https://efmaefm.org/0efmameetings/efma%20annual%20meetings/2009-milan/papers/corporate%20risk%20management%20and%20hedge%20accounting.pdf

Armstrong, S. May 1, 2014. *Smarter Than Us: The Rise of Machine Intelligence.*

Armstrong, S. September 16, 2015. *A Toy Model of the Control Problem*. Retrieved from https://lesswrong.com/posts/7cXBoDQ6udquZJ89c/a-toy-model-of-the-control-problem

Barrat, J. 2013. *Our Final Invention: Artificial Intelligence and the End of the Human Era.*

Bersohn, D., and L. McCree. July 26, 2018. *3 Steps to Reimagining your Tech Workforce in the AI Age*. Retrieved from https://cio.com/article/3293001/3-steps-to-reimagining-your-tech-workforce-in-the-ai-age.html

Bianculli, L. (n.d.). *10 Common IT Security Risks in the Workplace*. (managing director of enterprise and commercial sales at CCSI) Retrieved from https://ccsinet.com/blog/common-security-risks-workplace/

Bostrom, N. 2012. *The Superintelligent Will: Motivation and Instrumental Rationality in Advanced Artificial Agents*. (Future of Humanity Institute) Retrieved from https://nickbostrom.com/superintelligentwill.pdf

Bostrom, N. 2014. *Superintelligence: Paths, Dangers, Strategies.*

Branscombe, M. January 12, 2018. *How AI Could Revolutionize Project Management*. Retrieved from https://cio.com/article/3245773/project-management/how-ai-could-revolutionize-project-management.html

Branscombe, M. January 12, 2018. *How AI could revolutionize project management.* Retrieved from https://cio.com/article/3245773/how-ai-could-revolutionize-project-management.html

Bresnick, J. July 2016. *Predictive Big Data Analytics Identify High-Risk ED Patients.* Retrieved from https://healthitanalytics.com/news/predictive-big-data-analytics-identify-high-risk-ed-patients

Brownlee, J. November 25, 2013. *In Understand Machine Learning Algorithms.* Retrieved from https://machinelearningmastery.com/a-tour-of-machine-learning-algorithms/

Bruce, S. 2015. *Resources on Existential Risk.* Retrieved from https://futureoflife.org/data/documents/Existential%20Risk%20Resources%20(2015-08-24).pdf

Bryant, M. March 8, 2014. "Artificial Intelligence Could Kill Us All." *Meet the Man Who Takes that Risk Seriously.* Retrieved from https://thenextweb.com/insider/2014/03/08/ai-could-kill-all-meet-man-takes-risk-seriously/

Choudhary, A. November 19, 2018. *Reinforcement Learning: Introduction to Monte Carlo Learning using the OpenAI Gym Toolkit.* Retrieved from https://analyticsvidhya.com/blog/2018/11/reinforcement-learning-introduction-monte-carlo-learning-openai-gym/

Chowdhry, B., and J.T. Howe 1999. "Corporate Risk Management for Multinational Corporations: Financial and Operational Hedging Policies." *Review of Finance* 2, no. 2, pp. 229–246. Retrieved July 17, 2018, from http://anderson.ucla.edu/faculty/bhagwan.chowdhry/crm.pdf

Cindi Howson, J.R. February 11, 2019. *Magic Quadrant for Analytics and Business Intelligence Platforms.* Retrieved from https://gartner.com/doc/reprints?id=1-67X5TNE&ct=190212&st=sb

Columbus, L. May 9, 2016. *Ten Ways Big Data Is Revolutionizing Marketing And Sales.* Retrieved from https://forbes.com/sites/louiscolumbus/2016/05/09/ten-ways-big-data-is-revolutionizing-marketing-and-sales/#7c9cb40221cf

COOPER, S. March 7, 2019. *9 firms to watch in AI Cybersecurity.* (VPN News) Retrieved from https://comparitech.com/blog/information-security/leading-ai-cybersecurity-companies/

Cothenet, O. September 8, 2016. *10 Common Lies in Project Management—When Projects With a Green Light Status Fail.* Retrieved from https://projectmanagement.com/articles/343342/10-Common-Lies-in-Project-Management-When-Projects-With-a-Green-Light-Status-Fail

Cothenet, O. September 8, 2016. *10 Common Lies in Project Management—When Projects With a Green Light Status Fail.* Retrieved from https://projectmanagement.com/articles/343342/10-Common-Lies-in-Project-Management-When-Projects-With-a-Green-Light-Status-Fail

Delaney, K. June 2018. *AI and Security: the Arms Race.* Retrieved from https://connectedfutures.cisco.com/article/ai-security-arms-race/

Dformoso, D.F. (n.d.). *Machine-Learning-Mindmap*. (S. C. Google, Producer) Retrieved from https://github.com/dformoso/machine-learning-mindmap/blob/master/Machine%20Learning.pdf

Dhlamini, S.M., M.O. Kachienga, and T. Marwala. 2007. *Artificial Intelligence as an Aide in Management of Security Technology*. Retrieved July 17, 2018, from http://yadda.icm.edu.pl/yadda/element/bwmeta1.element.ieee-000004401470

Dvorsky, G. January 15, 2014. *Can We Build an Artificial Superintelligence that Won't Kill Us?* Retrieved from https://io9.gizmodo.com/can-we-build-an-artificial-superintelligence-that-wont-1501869007

Ericlicoding. December 18, 2017. *Machine Learning Algorithm Cheat Sheet for Azure Machine Learning Studio*. Retrieved from https://docs.microsoft.com/en-us/azure/machine-learning/studio/algorithm-cheat-sheet

Fallenstein, N.S. 2017. *Agent Foundations for Aligning Machine Intelligence with Human Interests: A Technical Research Agenda*. Retrieved from https://intelligence.org/files/TechnicalAgenda.pdf

Freeman, C.C. January 26, 2018. *Machine Learning and Security* (http://shop.oreilly.com/product/0636920065555.do ed.). oreilly.

Freeman, C.C. January 26, 2018. *Machine Learning and Security*. Retrieved from http://shop.oreilly.com/product/0636920065555.do

Friedman, E. October 2017. *Machine Learning Logistics*. Retrieved from https://learning.oreilly.com/library/view/machine-learning-logistics/9781491997628/

Ford, P. February 11, 2015. *Our Fear of Artificial Intelligence*. Retrieved from https://technologyreview.com/s/534871/our-fear-of-artificial-intelligence/

Furman, J. December 20, 2016. *Artificial Intelligence, Automation, and the Economy*. (Office of Science and Technology Policy) Retrieved from https://obamawhitehouse.archives.gov/sites/whitehouse.gov/files/documents/Artificial-Intelligence-Automation-Economy.PDF

Garyericson. March 4, 2019. *Machine Learning Algorithm Cheat Sheet for Azure Machine Learning Studio*. Retrieved from https://docs.microsoft.com/en-us/azure/machine-learning/studio/algorithm-cheat-sheet

Gold, J. October 2, 2017. *Key Considerations for Cyberrisk Coverage*. Retrieved from http://rmmagazine.com/2017/10/02/key-considerations-for-cyberrisk-coverage/

Gould, A. July 2, 2018. *From the Lab to the Top Line: How to turn cutting edge AI Research into Game Changing Products*. Retrieved from https://becominghuman.ai/from-the-lab-to-the-top-line-how-to-turn-cutting-edge-ai-research-into-game-changing-products-1136eec09efb

Grace, K. July 15, 2015. *The Asilomar Conference: A Case Study in Risk Mitigation*. (MIRI Research Assistant) Retrieved from https://intelligence.org/files/TheAsilomarConference.pdf

Group, I. A. 2017. *Artificial Intelligence in Energy and Utilities.* Retrieved from https://pin.it/7a26vjmc3blfvr

Guidry, P.E.E., D. Vaughn, R.P. Anderson, and J. Flores. September 2013. "Business Continuity and Disaster Management for Industrial Installations." Industry Applications Society 60th Annual Petroleum & Chemical Industry Conference. January 1, 2013. http://search.ebscohost.com/login.aspx?direct=true&AuthType=shib&db=edb&AN=92909986&site=eds-live (accessed August 25, 2019)

Haskell, W.H. May 17, 2018. *Stochastic Approximation for Risk-Aware Markov Decision Processes.* Retrieved from https://arxiv.org/pdf/1805.04238.pdf

Heathman, A. July 20, 2018. *Turn your Dancing into an AI-Powered GIF with Google's Move Mirror Experiment.* Retrieved from https://standard.co.uk/tech/google-move-mirror-dancing-gif-a3892471.html

Heldman, K. July 5, 1905. *Risk Management, Risk Analysis, Templates and Advice.* Retrieved from https://stakeholdermap.com/risk/risk-register.html

Hendry, E.R. January 21, 2014. *What Happens When Artificial Intelligence Turns On Us?* Retrieved from https://smithsonianmag.com/innovation/what-happens-when-artificial-intelligence-turns-us-180949415/

Hotzy, F. June 12, 2018. *Machine Learning: An Approach in Identifying Risk Factors for Coercion Compared to Binary Logistic Regression.* Retrieved from https://frontiersin.org/articles/10.3389/fpsyt.2018.00258/full

Hutson, M. July 27, 2018. *Artificial Intelligence has Learned to Probe the Minds of Other Computers.* (science journalist) Retrieved from https://sciencemag.org/news/2018/07/computer-programs-can-learn-what-other-programs-are-thinking?utm_medium=email&utm_source=topic+optin&utm_campaign=awareness&utm_content=20180730+ai+nl&mkt_tok=eyJpIjoi TmpFMVkyTTVaVFF5T0RObCIsInQiOiJCaWxXXNjFxZFdnSDdy RlwvMXRhRVV5YVFNdTZIU3Naelp3YVlyY0VRNFV5cXVqdCt 3a21aMHp2cytpUWxwT3JpZFwvSFN2c003SnRQU1VsNkhqa05 Cb2Q3Wndia0UyVk9pQmV4MnhURzd6cmFZR3pIa2RtVmM5 amF1Y2hyUUEwWlErIn0%3D

Institute, E.Y. 2008. *Artificial Intelligence as a Positive and Negative Factor in Global Risk.* Retrieved from http://intelligence.org/files/AIPosNegFactor.pdf

Internet Engineering Task Force. August 2007. *Internet Security Glossary,.* Retrieved from http://ietf.org/rfc/rfc4949.txt

ISO/IEC JTC1/SC27 (2008). Standing Document 6 (SD6):. March 19, 2008. *Glossary of IT Security Terminology.* Retrieved from http://jtc1sc27.din.de/sce/SD6

ITU-T, European Network and Information Security Agency (ENISA), Network and Information Security Steering Group (NISSG) (2007). (2007, September). *ICT Security Standards Roadmap, version 2.2.* Retrieved from http://itu.int/ITUT/studygroups/com17/ict/index.html

John P., and A.B. Holdren. October 12, 2016. *Preparing for the Future of Artificial Intelligence.* Retrieved from https://obamawhitehouse.archives.gov/sites/default/files/whitehouse_files/microsites/ostp/NSTC/preparing_for_the_future_of_ai.pdf

Journal of the American College of Cardiology. March 8, 2018. *Unsupervised Machine Learning Algorithm To Identify High and Low Risk Patients Following Crt Implantation.* Retrieved from http://onlinejacc.org/content/71/11_Supplement/A947

jsteinhardt. June 24, 2015. *Long-Term and Short-Term Challenges to Ensuring the Safety of AI Systems.* Retrieved from https://jsteinhardt.wordpress.com/2015/06/24/long-term-and-short-term-challenges-to-ensuring-the-safety-of-ai-systems/

Julia Hippisley-Cox, C. C. March 17, 2015. *Development and Validation of Risk Prediction Algorithms to Estimate Future Risk of Common Cancers in Men and Women: Prospective Cohort Study* . Retrieved from https://bmjopen.bmj.com/content/5/3/e007825

Katz, A. March 28, 2018. *Why are New York Taxi Drivers Killing Themselves?* Retrieved from https://wired.com/story/why-are-new-york-taxi-drivers-committing-suicide/

Knight, W. December 12, 2018. *Nine Charts that Really Bring Home Just How Fast AI is Growing.* Retrieved from https://technologyreview.com/s/612582/data-that-illuminates-the-ai-boom/

Kuepper, J. June 11, 2019. *How to Evaluate Country Risk for International Investing.* Retrieved from https://thebalance.com/how-to-evaluate-country-risk-1979203

Kumar, M. July 17, 2018. *21-Year-Old Creator of LuminosityLink Hacking Tool Pleads Guilty.* Retrieved from https://thehackernews.com/2018/07/luminositylink-hacking-tool.html?amp=1

Lanier, J. November 14, 2014. *The Myth Of AI.* Retrieved from https://edge.org/conversation/the-myth-of-ai#26015

Lee, E.G. February 24, 2015. *Pre-Competitive Collaboration in Pharma.* Retrieved from https://futureoflife.org/data/documents/PreCompetitiveCollaborationInPharmaIndustry.pdf

leonardoaraujosantos. (n.d.). *Markov Decision process.* Retrieved from https://leonardoaraujosantos.gitbooks.io/artificial-inteligence/content/markov_decision_process.html

Lipson, H. July 15, 2018. *Signing With Alexa: A DIY Experiment in AI Accessibility.* Retrieved from https://medium.com/syncedreview/signing-with-alexa-a-diy-experiment-in-ai-accessibility-57e4407af539

Luke. May 20, 2015. *A Reply to Wait But Why on Machine Superintelligence.* Retrieved from http://lukemuehlhauser.com/a-reply-to-wait-but-why-on-machine-superintelligence/

Lukeprog. March, 2012. *AI Risk and Opportunity: A Strategic Analysis.* Retrieved from https://lesswrong.com/posts/i2XoqtYEykc4XWp9B/ai-risk-and-opportunity-a-strategic-analysis

Magar, A. (Sphyrna Security). (n.d.). *State-of-the-Art in Cyber Threat Models and Methodologies.* Retrieved from http://cradpdf.drdc-rddc.gc.ca/PDFS/unc225/p803699_A1b.pdf

Magar, A. March, 2016. *State-of-the-Art in Cyber Threat Models and Methodologies.* (Sphyrna Security) Retrieved from http://cradpdf.drdc-rddc.gc.ca/PDFS/unc225/p803699_A1b.pdf

Mar, A. June 28, 2016. *130 Project Risks (List).* Retrieved from https://management.simplicable.com/management/new/130-project-risks

Mark, P., A. Özerdem, and S. Barakat. October 2002. "The Macro-Economic Impact of Disasters." *Progress in Development Studies* 2, no. 4, 283–305. doi:10.1191/1464993402ps042raPMI. 2017. A Guide to the Project Management Body of Knowledge (PMBOK® Guide) — 6th ed. and Agile Practice Guide (English)

Marsden, E. March 17, 2016. *The ISO 31000 standard on risk management: principles and guidelines.* (Programme manager at FonCSI) Retrieved from https://slideshare.net/EricMarsden1/the-iso-31000-standard-on-risk-management-principles-and-guidelines

Marsden, E. March 17, 2016. *The ISO 31000 standard on risk management: principles and guidelines.* (Programme manager at FonCSI) Retrieved from https://slideshare.net/EricMarsden1/the-iso-31000-standard-on-risk-management-principles-and-guidelines

Martin Reddy, P. July 29, 2018. *The 3 next steps in conversational AI.* Retrieved from https://venturebeat.com/2018/07/29/the-3-next-steps-in-conversational-ai/

Mateski, M., and C. M. Trevino. March 2012. *Cyber Threat Metrics.* Retrieved from https://fas.org/irp/eprint/metrics.pdf

McCarthy, J. 1959. *"Programs with Common Sense"* at the Wayback Machine (archived October 4, 2013). In *Proceedings of the Teddington Conference on the Mechanization of Thought Processes,* 756–791. London: Her Majesty's Stationery Office.

Miller, M. December 18, 2013. *Artificial intelligence, our final invention?* Retrieved from https://washingtonpost.com/opinions/matt-miller-artificial-intelligence-our-final-invention/2013/12/18/26ed6be8-67e6-11e3-8b5b-a77187b716a3_story.html

Morris, E. April 17, 2018. *3 of the Biggest Threats Facing Financial Institutions Today.* Retrieved from https://globalsign.com/en/blog/threats-to-financial-institutions-today/

Muehlhauser, L. 2012. *Intelligence Explosion: Evidence and Import.* Retrieved from http://intelligence.org/files/IE-EI.pdf

Muehlhauser, L. 2013. *Facing the Intelligence Explosion.*

Muehlhauser, L. May 2014. *Christof Koch and Stuart Russell on Machine Superintelligence.* Retrieved from https://intelligence.org/2014/05/13/christof-koch-stuart-russell-machine-superintelligence/

Mulgan, G. July 26, 2018. *10 Ways AI is a Force for Good.* (C. o. Nesta, Producer) Retrieved from https://medium.com/digital-leaders-uk/10-ways-ai-is-a-force-for-good-ee16e1937047

Newman, R. September 23, 2010. "US News." *How Netflix (and Blockbuster) Killed Block.* Retrieved from https://money.usnews.com/money/blogs/flowchart/2010/09/23/how-netflix-and-blockbuster-killed-blockbuster on September 22, 2019.

Nicole Perlroth, A.T. November 30, 2018. *Marriott Hacking Exposes Data of Up to 500 Million Guests.* Retrieved from https://nytimes.com/2018/11/30/business/marriott-data-breach.html

Panaretou, A., M.B. Shackleton, and P. Taylor. 2013. "Corporate Risk Management and Hedge Accounting." *Contemporary Accounting Research* 30, no. 1, pp. 116–139. Retrieved July 17, 2018, from http://efmaefm.org/0efmameetings/efma annual meetings/2009-milan/papers/corporate risk management and hedge accounting.pdf

Parnas, D.L. October 2017. *The Real Risks of Artificial Intelligence.* (Communications of the ACM,) Retrieved from https://cacm.acm.org/magazines/2017/10/221330-the-real-risks-of-artificial-intelligence/abstract

Powner, D.A. September 16, 2008. *Information Technology: Federal Laws, Regulations, and Mandatory Standards for Securing Private Sector Information Technology Systems and Data in Critical Infrastructure Sectors.* (Director, Information Technology Management Issues) Retrieved from https://gao.gov/assets/100/95747.pdf

Press, G. December 9, 2018. *120 AI Predictions For 2019.* Retrieved from https://forbes.com/sites/gilpress/2018/12/09/120-ai-predictions-for-2019/#5f5c10b1688c

Price, H. August 6, 2012. *Artificial Intelligence – Can We Keep It in the Box?* Retrieved from http://theconversation.com/artificial-intelligence-can-we-keep-it-in-the-box-8541

Productions, Shaking My Head. January 19, 2018. *Obsolete By 2030 - Humans Need Not Apply!* Retrieved from https://youtube.com/watch?v=GHc63Xgc0-8&feature=share

Raemon. February 2017. *What Should the Average EA Do About AI Alignment?* Retrieved from https://forum.effectivealtruism.org/posts/DkQaJwYMkSFN6E3f9/what-should-the-average-ea-do-about-ai-alignment

Reddy, M. July 29, 2018. *The 3 next steps in conversational AI.* Retrieved from https://venturebeat.com/2018/07/29/the-3-next-steps-in-conversational-ai/

Risk Management. (n.d.). *The Risk Management Process*. Retrieved from https://enisa.europa.eu/topics/threat-risk-management/risk-management/current-risk/risk-management-inventory/rm-process

Russell, S. April 29, 2014. *Transcendence : An AI Researcher Enjoys Watching His Own Execution*. Retrieved from https://huffpost.com/entry/ai-transcendence_b_5235364?guccounter=1

Russell, S. 2015. *What do you Think About Machines That Think?* Retrieved from https://edge.org/response-detail/26157

Santos, L. A. June 12, 2018. *Artificial Intelligence and Deep Learning*. Retrieved from https://leonardoaraujosantos.gitbooks.io/artificial-inteligence/content/markov_decision_process.html

Scheiber, N. July 7, 2018. *High-Skilled White-Collar Work? Machines Can Do That, Too*. Retrieved from https://nytimes.com/2018/07/07/business/economy/algorithm-fashion-jobs.html

Schiff, J.L. May 9, 2018. *5 Biggest IT Compliance Headaches and How to Address Them*. Retrieved from https://cio.com/article/2382445/compliance-7-biggest-it-compliance-headaches-and-how-cios-can-cure-them.html

Schmarzo, B. August 31, 2017. *Design Thinking: Future-Proof Yourself from AI*. Retrieved from https://datasciencecentral.com/profiles/blogs/design-thinking-future-proof-yourself-from-ai

Schmidt, M. July 3, 2018. *Build a Compelling Business Case*. Retrieved from https://business-case-analysis.com/

Schneier, B. 2015. *Resources on Existential Risk*. Retrieved from https://futureoflife.org/data/documents/Existential%20Risk%20Resources%20(2015-08-24).pdf

Security Executive Council. July 16, 2018. *A Risk Quantification Process*. Retrieved from https://securityexecutivecouncil.com/spotlight/?sid=30899

Segal, T. 2018. "Enron Scandal: The Fall of a Wall Street Darling." Retrieved from https://investopedia.com/updates/enron-scandal-summary/ on July 24, 2018.

Segal, T. May 29, 2019. *Enron Scandal: The Fall of a Wall Street Darling*. Retrieved from https://investopedia.com/updates/enron-scandal-summary/

Shirey. August 2007. *Internet Security Glossary, Version 2*. Retrieved from https://ietf.org/rfc/rfc4949.txt

Shulman, S.A. 2013. *Racing to the Precipice: a Model of Artificial Intelligence Development*. Retrieved from http://fhi.ox.ac.uk/wp-content/uploads/Racing-to-the-precipice-a-model-of-artificial-intelligence-development.pdf

Socher, C.M. April 3, 2017. *Lecture Collection | Natural Language Processing with Deep Learning* . (Stanford University School of Engineering) Retrieved from https://youtube.com/playlist?list=PL3FW7Lu3i5Jsnh1rnUwq_TcylNr7EkRe6

Spacey, J. November 29, 2015. *39 Examples of Project Risk*. Retrieved from https://simplicable.com/new/project-risk-examples

Spacey, J. January 2, 2017. *Business Guide*. Retrieved from https://simplicable. com/new/top

Stakeholdermap. (n.d.). *Project Management, Project Planning, Templates and Advice*. Retrieved from https://stakeholdermap.com/project-management/ project-management.html

Stakeholdermap. (n.d.). *Risk Management, Risk Analysis, Templates and Advice*. Retrieved from https://stakeholdermap.com/risk/risk-identification.html

Stedman, C. April, 2019. *Human-Like AI Quest Drives General AI development Efforts*. Retrieved from https://searchenterpriseai.techtarget.com/ essentialguide/Human-like-AI-quest-drives-general-AI-development-efforts

Stephen Hawking, M.T. June 19, 2014. *Transcending Complacency on Superintelligent Machines*. Retrieved from https://huffpost.com/entry/ artificial-intelligence_b_5174265

Synced. July 21, 2018. *Signing With Alexa: A DIY Experiment in AI Accessibility*. Retrieved from https://medium.com/syncedreview/signing-with-alexa-a-diy-experiment-in-ai-accessibility-57e4407af539

Tamar, A. June 1, 2015. *Risk-Sensitive and Efficient Reinforcement Learning Algorithms*. Retrieved from https://people.eecs.berkeley.edu/~avivt/phd_ thesis.pdf

Team, B. D. July 28, 2015. *89 KPIs in Risk Assessment Guide*. Retrieved from https://bscdesigner.com/risk-assessment-guide.htm

Tegmark, M. 2017. *Life 3.0: Being Human in the Age of Artificial Intelligence*.

Tom Everitt, G.L. May 3, 2018. *AGI Safety Literature Review*. Retrieved from https://arxiv.org/abs/1805.01109

Tomasik, B. April 10, 2018. *Artificial Intelligence and Its Implications for Future Suffering: Caring about the AI's Goals*. Retrieved from https://foundational-research.org/artificial-intelligence-and-its-implications-for-future-suffering

Tomasik, B. May 14, 2014. *Artificial Intelligence and Its Implications for Future Suffering*. Retrieved from https://foundational-research.org/artificial-intelligence-and-its-implications-for-future-suffering

Tuttle, H. November 2017. *Cybercrime Costs Businesses $11.7 Million Per Year*. Retrieved from http://rmmagazine.com/2017/11/01/cybercrime-costs-businesses-11-7-million-per-year/

Urban, T. January 22, 2015. *The AI Revolution: The Road to Superintelligence*. Retrieved from https://waitbutwhy.com/2015/01/artificial-intelligence-revolution-1.html

Vorhies, W. July 10, 2018. *What Makes a Successful AI Company—Data Dominance*. Retrieved from https://datasciencecentral.com/profiles/blogs/ what-makes-a-successful-ai-company

Vorhies, W. July 24, 2018. *Comparing AI Strategies – Systems of Intelligence*. Retrieved from https://datasciencecentral.com/profiles/blogs/comparing-ai-strategies-systems-of-intelligence

Wall Street Journal. May 2018. *Footage From Hawaii's Kilauea Volcano Eruption.* Retrieved from https://wsj.com/video/footage-from-hawaii-kilauea-volcano-eruption/E22D0275-52B3-4577-AB03-67B6040C7490.html

Watt, B. a. (n.d.). *Risk Management Planning.* Retrieved from https://opentextbc.ca/projectmanagement/chapter/chapter-16-risk-management-planning-project-management/

Watts, S. June 21, 2017. *IT Security Vulnerability vs Threat vs Risk: Understanding the Differences?* Retrieved from https://bmc.com/blogs/security-vulnerability-vs-threat-vs-risk-whats-difference/

Whittlestone, J. October 14, 2015. *Researchintorisksfromartificial Intelligence.*

Wolchover, N. April 21, 2015. *Concerns of an Artificial Intelligence Pioneer.* Retrieved from https://quantamagazine.org/artificial-intelligence-aligned-with-human-values-qa-with-stuart-russell-20150421

Xu, M. (Department of Mathematics Illinois State University, U.L.) March 2017. *Cybersecurity Insurance: Modeling and Pricing.* Retrieved from https://soa.org/Files/Research/Projects/cybersecurity-insurance-report.pdf

Xu, M., and A. Lei Hua. 2017. *Cybersecurity Insurance: Modeling and Pricing.* (Department of Mathematics,Illinois State University, USA. & Division of Statistics, Northern Illinois University, USA.) Retrieved from https://soa.org/globalassets/assets/Files/Research/Projects/cybersecurity-insurance-report.pdf

Yankoff, D. (n.d.). *Don't Confuse a Control Risk Assessment with Enterprise Risk Assessment.* Retrieved from http://tracerisk.com/category/functional-areas/

Yudkowsky, E., A. Salamon, C. Shulman, S. Kaas, T. McCabe, and R. Nelson. 2010. *Reducing Long-Term Catastrophic Risks from Artificial Intelligence.*

Yudkowsky, N.B. 2011. *The Ethics of Artificial Intelligence.* Retrieved from https://nickbostrom.com/ethics/artificial-intelligence.pdf

Yudkowsky, E. October 13, 2017. *There's No Fire Alarm for Artificial General Intelligence.* Retrieved from https://intelligence.org/2017/10/13/fire-alarm/

Zaharia, M. July 17, 2018. *MLflow: A Platform for Managing the Machine Learning Lifecycle.* Retrieved from https://oreilly.com/ideas/mlflow-a-platform-for-managing-the-machine-learning-lifecycle

About the Authors

Archie Addo:

Consultant, coach, author, and program/ project manager. Archie holds a PhD in Computer Information Systems (CIS) with an emphasis in e-commerce, cryptography, expert systems, and artificial intelligence. Dr. Addo has Executive Data Science Certification from Johns Hopkins University, a certificate in Contract Law from Harvard Law School, Harvard University, Certified Project Management Professional (PMP), Certified ScrumMaster (CSM), and Certified Scrum Product Owner (CSPO). With more than 20 years of experience in interrelated disciplines, Archie works with computer science, project management, procurement, organizational design and development, process engineering, quality management, and project team facilitation. He has held management positions including Software Development Manager, Consultant, and Senior Project Manager.

Archie is a subject matter expert (SME) reviewer for Global Congress and India Congress Project Management Institute (PMI) and is a contributor to PMI Risk Standard Management.

Srini Centhala:

Founder and Chief Architect of Absolut-e Data Com (a data company), providing expert consulting services to Fortune 100 companies (AT&T, Directv, Experian, eBay, and UPS) for more than 20 years and Chief Architect of BizStats Cloud Big Data AI Analytics platform. Centhala has designed and developed pricing engine, statistical modeling, prediction modeling, recommendation engine, text mining, sentiment analysis, data source analysis, and data science activities.

Specialties: Business process re-engineering, online business ideas, and concepts, business intelligence, technical architect/data architect/ data modeler in the business data management system, project management, and undertaking full projects, end to end. Srini applies machine learning and artificial intelligence to business data.

Muthu Shanmugam:

Chief Technology Officer at Absolut-e Data Com with more than 20 years of experience in all phases of the software development lifecycle. Shanmugam holds a Master of Engineering from Anna University, India. He has worked with various enterprise organizations as a dynamic leader of software development teams. Currently, Muthu works on Bizstats.ai, a knowledge-base-powered business intelligence and analytics cloud designed for businesses with limited BI resources. Key features include knowledge bases with numerous metrics and attributes for various industries, NLP-powered searches, dynamic reports, and dashboards. The company also features collaboration, which allows users to share reports and dashboards with their teams.

Index

OTHER TITLES IN THE BUSINESS LAW AND CORPORATE RISK MANAGEMENT COLLECTION

John Wood, Econautics Sustainability Institute, Editors

- *Preventing Litigation* by Nelson E. Brestoff and William H. Inmon
- *Buyer Beware* by Elvira Medici and Linda J. Spievack
- *Corporate Maturity and the "Authentic Company"* by David Jackman
- *Light on Peacemaking* by Thomas DiGrazia
- *Cybersecurity Law* by Shimon Brathwaite
- *Understanding Consumer Bankruptcy* by Scott B. Kuperberg

Announcing the Business Expert Press Digital Library

Concise e-books business students need for classroom and research

This book can also be purchased in an e-book collection by your library as

- a one-time purchase,
- that is owned forever,
- allows for simultaneous readers,
- has no restrictions on printing, and
- can be downloaded as PDFs from within the library community.

Our digital library collections are a great solution to beat the rising cost of textbooks. E-books can be loaded into their course management systems or onto students' e-book readers.
The **Business Expert Press** digital libraries are very affordable, with no obligation to buy in future years. For more information, please visit **www.businessexpertpress.com/librarians**. To set up a trial in the United States, please email **sales@businessexpertpress.com**.

CPSIA information can be obtained
at www.ICGtesting.com
Printed in the USA
FSHW021521081020
73923FS